CHILTON'S Repair and Maintenance Guide

Camper Trailers

ILLUSTRATED

Prepared by the

Automotive Editorial Department

Chilton Book Company
401 Walnut Street
Philadelphia, Pa. 19106
215—WA 5–9111

managing editor **JOHN D. KELLY;** assistant managing editor **PETER J. MEYER;** senior editor, recreational vehicle department, **KERRY A. FREEMAN;** editor **PHILIP A. CANAL;** technical editor **Robert J. Brown;** copy editor **Eric J. Roberts**

CHILTON BOOK COMPANY   PHILADELPHIA   NEW YORK   LONDON

Copyright © 1973 by Chilton Book Company

First Edition

Published in Philadelphia by Chilton Book Company
and simultaneously in Ontario, Canada,
by Thomas Nelson & Sons, Ltd.

Manufactured in the United States of America

Library of Congress Cataloging in Publication Data

Chilton Book Co. Automotive Editorial Dept.
   Chilton's repair and maintenance guide camper trailers.

    1. Campers and coaches, Truck—Maintenance and
repair.   I. Title.   II. Title: Repair and
maintenance guide: camper trailers.

| TL298.C47 | 1973 | 629.28′7′6 | 73-1023 |

ISBN 0-8019-5743-5
ISBN 0-8019-5851-2 (pbk)

Contents

ACKNOWLEDGEMENTS

CHILTON BOOK COMPANY expresses appreciation to the following firms for their assistance and technical information:

AIR LIFT COMPANY, Lansing, Michigan.

AIRSTREAM, Jackson Center, Ohio.

AMERICAN MOTORS CORPORATION, Detroit, Michigan.

ATWOOD VACUUM MACHINE COMPANY, Rockford, Illinois.

BERT R. PARKER & SONS, Glenolden, Pennsylvania.

CHEVROLET MOTOR DIVISION, GENERAL MOTORS CORPORATION, Lansing, Michigan.

CHRYSLER DIVISION, CHRYSLER MOTORS CORPORATION, Detroit, Michigan.

DICO, Moline, Illinois.

DODGE DIVISION, CHRYSLER MOTORS CORPORATION, Detroit, Michigan.

EQUAL-I-ZER SALES CORPORATION, South Salt Lake, Utah.

FAYETTE MANUFACTURING COMPANY, Fayette, Ohio.

FLEX-A-LITE CORPORATION, Tacoma, Washington.

FORD MARKETING CORPORATION, Dearborn, Michigan.

FRENCH & HECHT, a division of Kelsey-Hayes Company, Davenport, Iowa.

INTERTHERM, INCORPORATED, St. Louis, Missouri.

KELSEY-HAYES COMPANY, Mequon, Wisconsin.

OLDSMOBILE, a division of General Motors Corporation, Lansing, Michigan.

OWENS-CORNING FIBERGLASS CORPORATION, Toledo, Ohio.

PARDONNET MANUFACTURING COMPANY, INCORPORATED, Livonia, Michigan.

PONTIAC MOTOR DIVISION, GENERAL MOTORS CORPORATION, Pontiac, Michigan.

RECREATIONAL VEHICLE INSTITUTE, INC., Des Plaines, Illinois.

SERRO TRAVEL TRAILER COMPANY, Ashburn, Georgia.

THE COLEMAN COMPANY, INCORPORATED, Somerset, Pennsylvania.

THE TIMKEN COMPANY, Canton, Ohio.

WORTHINGTON CYLINDERS, Columbus, Ohio.

1 · General Information

Introduction

Since there is a tendency to confusion when speaking of the various classifications of travel trailers, let's begin with formal definitions for each variety of trailer.

The following are those definitions accepted by the Mobile Home Manufacturers Association. They define a Pickup Camper as a structure designed primarily to be mounted on a pickup or truck chassis of one-half ton or larger. There are two types of these units: slide-in campers (which are known as portable), and chassis-mount campers (which are permanently attached). Pickup Covers are similar but are portable and enclose the bed of

A chassis mount camper

pickup trucks providing all-weather protection. Other names for these units are caps and shells.

A Motor Home is a self-powered unit designed to provide complete living facilities. These include living and dining areas, usually a kitchen, and a full bath with a shower.

A Travel Trailer is a unit 10–35 ft long and 8 ft wide. These are designed to be towed behind passenger vehicles and may

A slide-in camper

A motor home

1

A travel trailer

able upper sections are usually made of canvas with either a canvas or fiberglass top.

The camper trailer is not totally self-sufficient. The usual sleeping capacity ranges from four to eight persons but household conveniences are lacking on smaller models. The larger ones sometimes offer interior lights, cooking facilities, a water supply, and storage space.

be constructed with either single or tandem axles. Trailers within this size range do not require special permits to be transported on public roads.

Camper Trailers are more compact, using a collapsible roof and sidewalls that can be raised quickly and folded out. When collapsed, the unit forms a neat outline which is ideal for towing and storage. Camper trailers are designed to be towed by an auto and are known also by the names of fold-down campers or tent trailers.

Camper trailers are constructed of light-weight aluminum or fiberglass and are mounted on a frame chassis. The mov-

A camper trailer in the closed position

A camper trailer in the open position

Preparing the Trailer for Use

If the trailer has been stored for a period of time, it is necessary to make a thorough check of all mechanical components before taking to the road. Lack of lubrication, corroded parts, or other malfunctions may cause irreparable damage if not corrected. Common sense dictates a thorough check before using the trailer.

The following chart is a good checklist to follow when returning a stored trailer to service.

1. Check the condition of both tires and tire rims. Also check the lug nuts for the correct (manufacturer's) torque.

2. Make an inspection of the wheel bearings for condition and lubrication. It is a good idea to repack the bearings a few times each season, depending on trailer mileage.

3. Check the trailer's braking system (if equipped). This must be a thorough check since it is the most critical part of a trailer's components. Inspect the linings, drums, and hydraulic lines. Check the fluid, line connections, and wheel cylinders for any sign of leaks.

4. Lubricate all points recommended by the factory—with the recommended lubricant.

5. Examine the hitch tongue for any cracks or stress tears.

6. Check the electrical lines for positive connections and loose wires which might contact the frame.

7. Fill the tires to the recommended pressure.

HITCHING THE TRAILER TO THE TOW VEHICLE

1. Make sure all the breakables are secured before the tent trailer is collapsed. If

the walkway sections of the trailer are used for storage, make sure that all items are secure to prevent breakage.

2. Make certain that all cabinet doors are closed and that the door (if so equipped) is secured correctly. Also remember to secure the retractable steps if your unit is so equipped.

3. Raise the hitch ball until the coupler of the trailer is high enough to clear the hitch ball on the tow vehicle.

Positioning the hitch ball under the coupler (© Airstream Corp.)

4. Back the tow vehicle to the trailer or move the trailer to the vehicle—whichever is easier. Position the coupler onto the hitch ball, making sure that it is securely placed and that the handle is set into the lock position. Also place a bolt through the coupler handle as an added safety feature.

Lowering the coupler onto the hitch ball and securing the lock. (© Airstream Corp.)

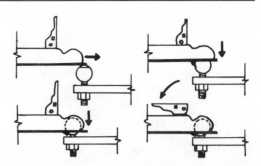

Hitch ball and coupler positions during hitching up.

5. If the trailer is equipped with an equalizing hitch, position the equalizing bars in their correct positions by placing chains on the equalizing bars onto the same links on both sides of the tongue. Stand back from the trailer and the tow vehicle to see if the tow vehicle is leaning to the front. If it is, the equalizer chains must be lowered one notch.

6. Attach the safety chains and the breakaway switch to the tow vehicle. (See the brake section.)

7. Remove the front jack and retract the dolly wheel (if so equipped).

8. Attach the electrical connections from the tow vehicle to the trailer and then test the lights to see if all the directional signals, stop lights, and back-up lights work correctly.

9. Make a quick test of the trailer brakes to see if they operate correctly without any drag or noise.

OFF-SEASON STORAGE AND WINTERIZING

When the trailer is not to be used for an extended period of time, it should be stored in the correct manner.

Jack the trailer wheels individually and place them on wooden blocks so the mois-

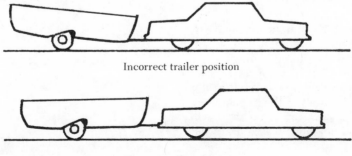

Incorrect trailer position

Correct trailer position

Trailer dolly wheel

ture from the ground will not rot the tires. If desired, the wheel and tire may be removed and stored in a cool, dry place. If jacking the trailer is an inconvenience, all you have to do is back the trailer onto the blocks. The jacking procedure is best however, because holding the trailer up by jacks removes all the weight from the suspension. This affords the springs and shock absorbers optimum life expectancy.

The main concern in winterizing is to protect your hot and cold water systems, including the traps, waste holding tank, water heater, and battery, from freezing. You should use the same precautions that you would use in your home if you were to go away for an extended period of time during the winter. Keep this in mind while you follow the directions listed below.

1. Level the trailer from side to side and from front to rear. Open all of the faucets.

2. Turn off the water pump.

3. Open all of the drain valves for the water tank, the hot water heater, and the holding tank. Open any valve that might be located in the middle of a line.

4. Lower the front of the trailer as far as the tongue jack will allow. When water ceases to drain from all of the open valves, crank the tongue jack up as far as it will go and let the remaining water drain out of the trailer.

5. After the water has stopped flowing

from the drains, apply air pressure, if at all possible, to the drain lines with all drain valves and faucets open.

6. Pour a cup of Glycol type antifreeze into the sink and tub drains to prevent water from freezing in the traps.

7. Open the waste holding tank drain and flush the tank thoroughly. This is very important because frozen waste in the tank could cause serious damage.

8. Remove the inlet and outlet lines on the water pump and turn the pump by hand until all of the water is removed.

9. Remove the battery from the trailer, (if equipped) and store it in a place where it won't freeze—preferably your house. Do not store the battery in contact with the ground or on a concrete floor. Put blocks of wood under it or place it on a workbench so the battery cannot establish a ground and drain itself of all electrical power. If a battery is allowed to go completely dead, it will probably not accept a charge; if it does, it will not come up to its original power rating. The battery should be charged at regular intervals throughout the winter to ensure a full charge in the spring.

10. Remove any food, cosmetics, or other items from the trailer that might be damaged by freezing or might damage the trailer if their containers break.

An aftermarket additive named "Winterize" can be added to your trailer's water system, including the drinking water tank, to protect against freezing. The liquid itself is guaranteed to be efficient to −60° F and has been warranted safe for human consumption by the federal government.

Winterize is added to the tank with the necessary amount of water to dilute it to the proper freezing range. This is tested much the same as is car antifreeze, with a suction gauge. The chart shows the proper combination of Winterize and water to gain the proper freezing levels.

Winterize (gal concentrate)	Water Dilution (qt)	Approx. Protection (°F)
1	0	−60
1	1	−56
1	2	−50
1	3	−30 to −23
1	4 (1 gal)	−20 to −12
1	5	−10 to −4
1	6	−3 to 0
1	7	0 to 4
1	8 (2 gal)	5 to 9

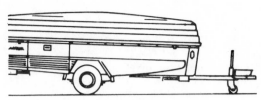

Camper in the folded position

Although the red color of "Winterize" may be present in the water, the manufacturer recommends use of the tester to ensure proper consistency.

Travel with the Trailer

CHECKLIST FOR THE ROAD

While it is impossible to be prepared for every possible emergency, it is possible to overcome most of the day-to-day tragedies. The following is a small list of equipment which can be helpful in an emergency.

1. First aid kit
2. Fire extinguisher (dry chemical type)
3. Assortment of common tools
4. Tow rope (35–50 ft)
5. Jack and correct size of lug wrench
6. Spare tire, properly inflated
7. Distress flares
8. Flashlight
9. Sewer hose with campground connections (if the camper is equipped with a holding tank)
10. Three-prong electrical extension cord (100 ft) with two prong adaptors
11. Small shovel and axe
12. Bucket and trailer type water hose (50 ft)

PARKING THE TRAILER

Maneuvering a camper trailer behind your car can be tricky business for a novice. With a reasonable amount of practice, however, a person with an average amount of driving ability can master it.

Practice in a large area with ample room for both left-hand and right-hand turns. Turn slowly and watch the tracking of the trailer as compared to the tracking of the tow vehicle. The trailer can be seen by using truck type rear-view mirrors mounted to the doors or fenders of the tow vehicle. These mirrors are required in most states.

Backing the trailer is the hardest maneu-

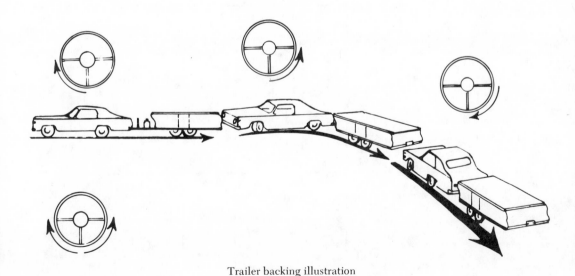

Trailer backing illustration

ver to learn. It is most important to back slowly. The basic procedure is to watch the rear of the trailer and get it going in the desired direction first. When both car and trailer are in a straight line, turn the steering wheel in the direction you wish the trailer to go, then turn the wheel in the reverse direction with the car following in the same arc as the trailer.

When first learning to back a trailer, place one hand at the bottom of the steering wheel. From this position, the direction of hand movement will be the direction of trailer movement. If your hand moves to the left, the trailer will move to the left; if your hand moves to the right, the trailer will move to the right. This is a good practice for a novice to follow.

No matter what type of hitch you buy, even the best cannot eliminate the swaying of the trailer when it is passed by a large truck or bus. The air being displaced by the truck or bus first pushes the back and then the front of the trailer. You should not apply the brakes on either the trailer or the tow vehicle. Instead, steer very slightly, and momentarily, toward the bus or truck just as the trailer starts to sway. This will compensate for the sway that is induced by the passing vehicle.

SECURING THE TRAILER

Once the trailer is properly parked, place chocks on the trailer wheels to prevent it from moving. Once the wheels are blocked, lower the corner jacks (usually four—one on each corner). Place a piece of wood 6 in. square by ¾ in. thick under each jack to keep it from sinking into the ground. Level the trailer with corner jacks.

Corner jack

The combination of the trailer's suspension and the corner jacks will make the average camper trailer most stable and comfortable.

State and Provincial Trailer Laws

RULES FOR THE ROAD
FOR TRAVEL TRAILERS AND OTHER RECREATIONAL VEHICLES

Note: Contact State Police for Changes to Laws and Regulations. State or Province	Speed Limits (mph)① Day	Night	Business	Residential	Maximum Dimensions Length⑪	Width	Height	Required Equipment Brakes, if Weight is Over:	Safety Chains	Stop Light	Tail Light	Clearance Light	License Light	Reflectors	Flares	Turn Signals	Other	Riding Permitted in Trailer	Overnight Off-Roadway Parking Allowed⑬
Alabama	60-70	50-60	20	25	55'	8'	13'6"			°	°	°	°	°		°	㉒	Yes	②
Alaska	50-70	50-70	25	25	60'	8'	13'6"	3000	°	°	°	°	°	°	°	°		No	Yes
Arizona	65	60	25	25	65'	8'	13'6"	1500	°	°	°	°	°		°			No	Yes
Arkansas	60	60	30	30	60'	8'	13'6"	3000	°	°	°	°		°	°	°		No	Yes
California	55	55	25	25	60'	8'	13'6"	1500	°	°	°	°	°	°	°	°		No	Yes⑫
Colorado	60-70	60-70	35	35	65'	8'	13'6"	1500	°	°	°	°	°		°			No	No
Connecticut	60-70	AP	AP	AP	50'	8'6"	13'6"	3000	°	°	°	°	°					No	No
Delaware	AP	AP	AP	AP	65'	8'	13'6"	2000	°	°	°	°	°	°	°	°	㉒	No	Yes

State and Provincial Trailer Laws (cont.)

RULES FOR THE ROAD
FOR TRAVEL TRAILERS AND OTHER RECREATIONAL VEHICLES

Note: Contact State Police for Changes to Laws and Regulations.

State or Province	Speed Limits (mph)① Day	Night	Business	Residential	Length⑪	Width	Height	Brakes, if Weight is Over:	Safety Chains	Stop Light	Tail Light	Clearance Light	License Light	Reflectors	Flares	Turn Signals	Other	Riding Permitted in Trailer	Overnight Off-Roadway Parking Allowed⑬
District of Columbia	25	25	25	25	50'	8'	12'6"	3000	•	•	•		•					No	No
Florida	AP	AP	AP	AP	55'	8'	13'6"	3000	•	•	•	•	•	•	•	•		No	Yes⑥
Georgia	60-70	50-65	35	35	55'	8'	13'6"	2500	•	•	•	•	•	•	•		㉒	No	Yes
Hawaii	25-65	25-65	25	25	65'	9'	13'6"	1500		•	•	•						Yes	No
Idaho	60	55	AP	AP	60'	8'	14'	3000		•	•		•	•	•			Yes	Yes
Illinois	55	55	30	30	60'	8'	13'6"	3000	•	•	•			•	•			No	Yes⑫
Indiana	65	65	AP	AP	55'	8'	13'6"	3000	•	•	•		•					Yes	Yes
Iowa	55-75	55-65	20	25	60'	8'	13'6"	⑤	•	•	•	•	•		•			Yes	No
Kansas	70	60	20	30	50'	8'	13'6"	⑤	•	•	•		•	•			㉒	No	No③
Kentucky	60	50	AP	AP	55'	8'	13'6"	⑤	⑤	•	•		•	•	•			Yes	Yes④
Louisiana	60-70	60-70	AP	AP	60'	8'	13'6"	3000	•	•	•	•	•			•		No	Yes⑤
Maine	45 AP	45 AP	AP	AP	55'	8'6"	13'6"		•	•	•	•	•					No	No
Maryland	AP	AP	AP	AP	55'	8'	13'6"	1500	•	•	•	•	•					No	Yes⑥
Massachusetts	50	50	30	30	⑮	8'⑭	13'6"	⑯	•	•	•		•			•		No	No
Michigan	50	50	25	25	60'	8'4"	12'6"	1500	•	•	•	•	•			•	㉒	Yes	No
Minnesota	65	55	30	30	55'	8'	13'6"	1500	•	•	•	•	•	•	•			No	No
Mississippi	65	65	AP	AP	55'	8'	13'6"	2000	•	•	•	•	•	•				Yes	Yes
Missouri	65-70	60-70	AP	AP	55'	8'	13'6"	No		•	•		•	•		•		No	Yes
Montana	50	50	AP	AP	60'	8'	13'6"	3000		•	•	•		•				Yes	Yes
Nebraska	50	50	20	25	65'	8'	13'6"	All		•	•	•						No	Yes⑦
Nevada	AP	AP	AP	AP	55'	8'	Any	3000	•	•	•	•	•					No	No
New Hampshire	45	45	AP	AP	55'	8'	13'6"	3000	•	•	•	⑰	•	⑰	⑰	⑰	㉒	Yes	Yes
New Jersey	50	50	25	25	45'	8'	13'6"	3000	•	•	•		•		•	•		No	Yes⑤
New Mexico	60	50	25	25	65'	8'	13'6"	3000		•	•	•						No	No
New York	50	50	AP	AP	55'	8'	13'6"	1000		•	•	•	•		•			No	Yes
North Carolina	45	45	20	35	55'	8'	13'6"	1000	•	•	•	•	•		•	•		No	Yes
North Dakota	60	60	25	25	60'	8'	13'6"	All	•	•	•		•	•		•		Yes	No
Ohio	60-70	50	25	35	60'	8'	13'6"	2000	•	•	•	•	•	•	•	•		Yes	No
Oklahoma	50-70	50	AP	AP	55'	8'	13'6"	3000	•	•	•	•	•	•	•			Yes	Yes
Oregon	55	55	20	25	60'	8'	13'6"	⑨	•	•	•	•	•	•	•			No	No
Pennsylvania	55-60	55-60	AP	AP	55'	8'	13'6"	3000	•	•	•	•	•		•			No	Yes
Rhode Island	50	45	25	25	55'	8'6"	13'6"	4000		•	•	•	•					No	No
South Carolina	55-70	50-65	25	30	60'	8'	13'6"	3000	•	•	•	•	•		•			Yes	Yes
South Dakota	70	60	30	30	60'	8'	13'6"	3000		•	•	•		•				Yes	No
Tennessee	50-75	50-75	AP	AP	55'	8'	13'6"	1500		•	•	•		•	•			Yes	Yes
Texas	⑱	⑱	AP	AP	55'	8'	13'6"	3000		•	•	•	•	•				Yes	Yes
Utah	AP	AP	25	25	60'	8'	14'	2000	•	•	•	•	•		•		㉓	No	Yes
Vermont	50	50	AP	AP	55'	8'	13'6"	1500	•	•	•	•	•		•			No	Yes
Virginia	45-55⑲	45-55⑲	AP	AP	55'	8'	13'6"	3000	•	•	•	•	•	•				Yes	No
Washington	⑳	⑳	25	25	65'	8'	13'6"	㉑	•	•	•	•	•	•	•			No	No
Wisconsin	65	55	AP	AP	60'	8'	13'6"	3000		•	•	•	•	•		•		Yes	Yes⑤
West Virginia	55-70	55-70	25	25	55'	8'	12'6"	3000	•	•	•	•	•	•	•	•		Yes	Yes④
Wyoming	65-75	65-75	20	30	65'	8'	13'6"	3000	•	•	•	•	•	•				Yes	Yes
Alberta	AP	AP	AP	AP	65'	8'6"	12'6"	2000	•	•	•	•	•	•				No	⑩
British Columbia	50	50	AP	AP	60'	8'	12'6"	3000	•	•	•	•	•					No	No
Manitoba	60	60	30	30	65'	8'6"	13'6"	10,000	•	•	•	•	•					No	Yes
New Brunswick	60	60	30	30	60'	8'6"	13'6"	3000		•	•	•	•	•	•		㉒	No	Yes
Newfoundland	AP	AP	AP	AP	55'	8'	12'6"	6000		•	•	•	•					No	⑩

State and Provincial Trailer Laws (cont.)

RULES FOR THE ROAD
FOR TRAVEL TRAILERS AND OTHER RECREATIONAL VEHICLES

Note: Contact State Police for Changes to Laws and Regulations. State or Province	Speed Limits (mph)①				Maximum Dimensions			Required Equipment											Riding Permitted in Trailer	Overnight Off-Roadway Parking Allowed⑬
	Day	Night	Business	Residential	Length⑪	Width	Height	Brakes, if Weight is Over:	Safety Chains	Stop Light	Tail Light	Clearance Light	License Light	Reflectors	Flares	Turn Signals	Other		
Northwest Territories	60	60	AP	AP	60'	8'	13'6"	1500	°	°	°	°	°	°	°	°		No	⑩
Nova Scotia	60	60	30	30	65'	8'6"	13'	4000		°	°	°	°	°	°	°		Yes	Yes⑧
Ontario	50	50	30	30	65'	8'6"	13'6"	2999	°	°	°	°	°	°		°		No	Yes⑫
Prince Edward Island	60	55	30	40	80'	8'6"	14'6"	8000		°	°	°	°			°		Yes	Yes
Quebec	50	45	30	30	60'	8'6"	12'6"	3000	°	°	°	°	°	°	°	°	㉒	No	No
Saskatchewan	65	60	AP	AP	65'	8'6"	13'6"	3000		°	°		°		°			No	Yes④
Yukon	60 AP	60 AP	AP	AP	70'	8'6"	13'6"	1500	°	°	°	°	°	°	°		㉒	No	Yes

Notes:

AP As Posted

① Posted speed limits always take precedence over statutory speed limits
② Not at roadside parks
③ Yes in rest areas with toilets
④ Not at roadside parks and rest areas
⑤ Recommended but not required
⑥ Not on limited access or state highways
⑦ In rural areas, not on state highways
⑧ At rest areas
⑨ Trailers over 45'
⑩ Only in designated areas
⑪ Trailer and towing vehicle without permit
⑫ Except when otherwise posted
⑬ Parking never allowed along limited access expressways or freeways, except when indicated above at rest areas

⑭ Additional 6" is allowed for mirrors
⑮ Maximum length for travel trailer without permit is 33'
⑯ Brakes not required if towing vehicle foot brakes will stop from 20 mph within 30', and hand brake within 80'
⑰ Required on vehicles 80" or more in width
⑱ 60 mph day and 55 mph night if overall length is 32' or less, excluding tow bar or weight less than 4500 lbs; otherwise 45 mph
⑲ Same as passenger cars if trailer weight does not exceed 2500 lbs
⑳ Truck speed limits when towing, generally 10 mph less than passenger cars
㉑ Required if weight of trailer exceeds 3000 lbs or 40 per cent of towing vehicle
㉒ Safety glass
㉓ Fire extinguisher

2 · Tow Vehicle and Hitches

Types of Tow Vehicles

With the epidemic growth of trailers—especially the less expensive camper trailers—car manufacturers have recently offered an option known as the "Trailer Package." This option includes such components as a larger engine, over-sized alternator and radiator, heavy-duty shock absorbers and springs, heavy-duty transmission and transmission oil cooler, larger radiator fan, and a radiator shroud. Now, instead of adding all of the advantageous aftermarket components, the car can be ordered with these items as factory equipment.

The total weight-to-horsepower ratio is very important for cars which will be used as tow vehicles. The most practical upper limit is approximately 60 lbs per horsepower while the average is 30–40 lbs/hp. The ratio is calculated by adding the weight of the trailer and the tow vehicle, and then dividing by the rated engine horsepower. One must remember that the weight of the provisions in the trailer must be considered in the calculations.

EFFECTS OF PULLING ON THE TOW VEHICLE

The increased weight of the trailer obviously affects the tow vehicle. One can only estimate the exact relationship between driving with the trailer and without it but some effects are certain; the acceleration time increased and gas mileage is reduced. Grade climbing ability and top speed are also reduced.

Remember that you need more time to accelerate when you are towing a trailer.

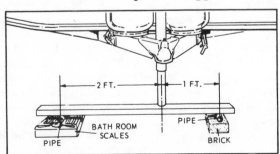

To check the trailer tongue weight use a brick and a bathroom scale of approximately the same thickness and construct the weighing mechanism as shown. A 2 x 4 or a 4 x 4 can be used to support the trailer. To calculate the correct tongue weight multiply the reading of the scale by three.

You must also allow for the increased length of the trailer when returning to the right-hand lane.

FACTORS AFFECTING TOWING

When purchasing a tow vehicle, keep in mind the approximate vicinity where it will be used. Both climate and temperature greatly affect performance. For example, a unit which is set to run on the eastern coast of the United States will have to be modified to run correctly in the mountainous West were the air is thinner.

The advantages of transmission coolers and oversized radiators are apparent if the unit is to run in a warm climate.

Since no one is expected to stay at home with his trailer rig, it is best to fit the vehicle with warm-weather as well as cold-weather equipment and deal with thin-air problems as they arise. Any qualified mechanic can make the adjustments necessary for mountainous driving.

Vehicle Safety

SAFE ROUTES AND SPEEDS

The key words are "plan ahead." Some of us like surprises but most don't. When planning a camping trip, sit down with up-to-date maps and plan the safest, most convenient route because it is no fun getting lost. Also calculate the distance to be covered during each day so you can find the approximate location of each night's campsite. This will enable you to make reservations for your campsites ahead of time, saving time and trouble searching after a full day of driving.

Speed recommendations are always relative. They are dependent on the size and weight of the trailer and the tow vehicle, and the braking and acceleration ability of the unit together. Common sense is perhaps most important. Remember that as your speed increases, so does the instability of the trailer, causing greater control problems. Today's trailers advertise cruising speeds equal to most driving needs but there are so many variables (e.g., wind and terrain) that maintaining a reasonable speed is important. Also the faster you go, the more horsepower is needed just to

overcome the greater wind resistance created by the trailer. Thus the less miles per gallon of gas you receive from the tow vehicle. Your most economical cruising speed can be determined only through trial and error.

TRAILER SAFETY CHAINS

The safety chain is a link between the trailer frame and the bumper or frame of the car. These chains keep the trailer from separating from the car if the hitch or hitch connection breaks. They are mandatory equipment in some states.

The safety chain should be attached to the trailer frame and to the car bumper or frame with a tight connection. Make sure the connection is tight; if it breaks, the chain will keep the hitch tongue from striking the ground. The safety chain is a good precaution against a breakaway trailer and the damage it could cause.

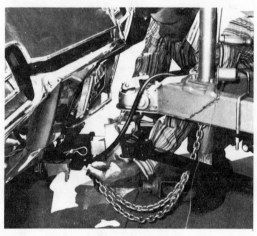

Safety chains (© Airstream Corp.)

PERIODIC INSPECTION OF THE TOW VEHICLE

Examine the tow vehicle before towing the trailer any great distance. Follow the paragraphs below in checking the car components.

Inspect the hitch assembly. Check for any stress cracks in the hitch supports or any loose welds or broken bolts. In short, make certain that the hitch is still securely attached to the tow vehicle.

A common and troublesome mistake is buying a larger trailer and attempting to use the same hitch. This can cause permanent damage to the car as well as the trailer and possibly an accident. See that the new trailer and its hitch are made for each other (within the same weight classification). It is less hazardous to replace a larger trailer with a smaller one without changing the hitch. The only possible result of this will be overstiffness of the hitch.

Check the car's shock absorbers by pushing down on that part of the body above the shock. Continue pushing until the car is moving up and down briskly, then stop the pressure. If the vehicle keeps bobbing, the shock is bad. The car should return to the rest position within one bounce of the car. Check the shocks for leakage and replace them as necessary.

Tow vehicle shock absorbers should be replaced every 10,000 miles at a maximum. Faulty shocks can greatly increase the twisting motion of the car body, causing harder handling and magnifying the possibilities of an accident.

Inspect the tow vehicle tires before any trip. They should be in good condition and should all have equal pressure. Using recapped tires or snow tires in the summer season is only asking for trouble. Also, alternating an old tire with a new one on the rear of the car may cause trouble in stopping or even jackknifing.

The above list, as small as it might seem, is of great importance. It is, however, not the end of the inspection. Inspect all the mechanical components of the car yourself or have this done by a qualified mechanic. Such things as lubricant in the crankcase and in the transmission should be checked along with the cooling system level and front-end alignment. Have these things attended to so that a breakdown will not hamper your free time.

Tow Vehicle Components

SPRINGS

Overload springs are added to the stock equipment to raise the rear of the vehicle to the normal, level driving position when the trailer is attached. Overload springs come in a variety of models, ranging from coil springs to leaf spring sets which are added to the factory equipment.

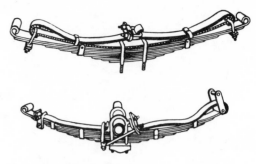

Two types of overload springs

With the advent of air-lift shock absorbers and air bag spring inserts, overload springs are rarely used except on older vehicles. They do, however, give the correct position to the car which otherwise, because of the weight, would be sitting with

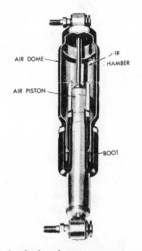

A superlift shock absorber

Air bag spring insert

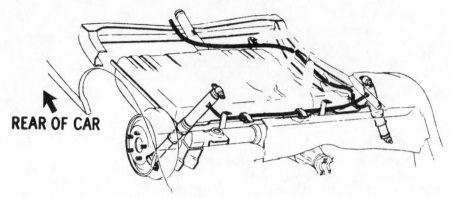

REAR OF CAR

Airshock and pressure line location on the tow vehicle

its nose high in the air. This nose-up position leads to hazardous driving. Since all the weight is transferred to the rear axle and none is left on the front suspension for steering, this condition results in unpredictable handling and extreme tire wear.

Driving at night with the car in a nose-up position is dangerous because your headlights are, in effect, improperly aimed. They are too high, shining into the eyes of oncoming drivers and making it difficult for them to see properly. You also won't be able to see the road surface the way you should.

LIMITED-SLIP DIFFERENTIAL

Since the traction of the tow vehicle plays such an important part in driving and towing, anything to help is an asset. The limited-slip or positive traction rear axle falls into this category.

Conventional "open" differentials have a tendency to transfer the torque of the engine to the rear wheel with the least resistance. When the left rear wheel is on ice and the right rear wheel is on dry surface, the force of the engine causes, the left rear wheel to spin freely; the car can gain no traction. The limited-slip differential has an internal clutching system which transfers the torque from the spinning wheel to the wheel which has the most resistance, thus enabling the vehicle to move forward.

This type of differential is a definite advantage in foul weather (e.g., snow and rain). Remember that the traction of the tow vehicle is of utmost importance for safety. Limited-slip or positive traction rear axles were available for many years as an option on standard cars. Today they come as standard equipment on most cars intended for towing.

To check for this locking differential, jack up the rear of the car so the two rear wheels clear the ground. Spin either tire in the direction of forward movement and watch the rotation of the other tire. If the other tire turns in the same direction as the one you are turning, the differential is a clutch type differential; if the other tire turns in the reverse direction, the axle is an open type.

TRANSMISSIONS

Manual

The manual transmission, or "stick" was previously thought to be the "most reliable" type of transmission for towing. The positive contact of the clutch disc to the flywheel gives a positive engagement. Recently, however, a closer examination of the clutch mechanism for towing has come about. When you think about how the clutch works, you can see its disadvantages.

The idea of a clutch type transmission is positive engagement with a limited amount of slip. When towing a reasonably large camper with a medium-sized engine, however, the driver must slip the clutch greatly in order to get the car to move initially. Once moving, positive engagement is allowable. You can easily see this problem magnified on a slippery surface. In order to set the vehicle and trailer into motion, the clutch must be slipped drastically. If it is not, the wheels will spin freely because of the sudden application of torque on the slippery surface.

Automatic

With the advent of the new Turbo-Hydra-matic, and other modern three-speed transmissions, old wives' tales about automatics for towing have fallen by the wayside. In fact, the trailer towing packages available from the large manufacturers recommend the automatic transmission.

Older automatics lived up to the fears of trailer towers mainly because the car itself was not set up for towing. Either the differential was of an incorrect ratio or the car wasn't driven correctly. In order to function correctly, the vehicle must be geared to tow. This point will be discussed in the "Rear Axle Ratio" section.

The advantage of the automatic transmission, as opposed to the manual, is that the torque may be applied gradually without any slipping. The slip of the torque converter accomplishes this action. This is not the type of slip as in a clutch set-up because there is no wear to any components. The gradual starting procedure allows gradual transfer of torque to the rear wheels and lessens the chance of the wheels breaking free.

Automatic Transmission Oil Cooling

Transmission oil coolers are usually offered with the automobile manufacturer's new trailer towing packages since the transmission has to work harder to overcome the extra load of a trailer than it does normally. The extra load causes the transmission to create more heat due to increased friction and the extra heat is transferred to the transmission oil. If the oil is allowed to become too hot, it will change its chemical compo_ition or become burnt. Valve bodies then become clogged and the transmission doesn't operate as efficiently as it should. Serious damage to the transmission can result. Thus the need for the extra transmission oil cooling capacity.

You can tell if the transmission fluid is burnt by inspecting it for a burnt smell and discoloration. Burnt transmission fluid

is dark brown or black as opposed to its normal bright red color. Burnt transmission fluid will also have a distinct, burnt order. Since the fluid "cooks" in stages, it may develop sludge or varnish. It is also possible for a leak to develop inside the radiator oil cooler and contaminate the transmission fluid. Pull out the transmission dipstick and place the end on a tissue or paper towel. Particles of sludge can be seen easier this way. If any of the above conditions exist, the transmission fluid should be completely drained, the filtering screens cleaned, the transmission inspected for possible damage, and new fluid installed.

The solution to these problems, as mentioned previously, is the installation of a transmission oil cooler which you can buy at any well-supplied auto parts store or trailer service center.

An additional benefit of installing a transmission oil cooler is that the engine block will also run cooler since some of the cooling load will be removed from the water-cooling radiator.

Do not install the oil-cooling radiator in

Oil cooler components

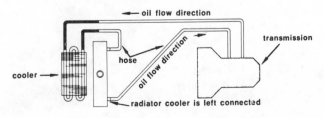

Diagram of the transmission cooling system

front of the water-cooling radiator; it will restrict the flow of air through the water-cooling radiator.

Proper driving techniques can also help to keep the transmission oil cool when towing a trailer. Do not lug the engine in high gear at low speeds. Downshift the transmission into the next lower gear. This reduces the heat from the transmission by increasing the mechanical efficiency of the torque convertor. The engine cooling capacity is also increased due to higher fan and water pump rpm.

REAR AXLE RATIO VARIATIONS

The rear axle ratio is very important to a vehicle which is used to tow a trailer. The average car as it comes straight from the factory has a rear axle ratio suited to a car which is to be used under normal load conditions. Such vehicles are equipped with differential ratios in the high twos, such as a 2.73 ratio.

The axle ratio is the relationship between the number of turns the driveshaft makes as compared with the number of turns of the drive axles. For example, if the car is equipped with a 2.73 differential, the driveshaft will turn 2.73 times for each time the drive axles turn once. It would then be said that this car has a 2.73:1 differential. This drive axle ratio, with the size of the engine, determines the pulling power of the car.

There is no recommended differential ratio which is a set figure and will cover all trailers. A 3.63 ratio can be used with a six-cylinder engine effectively while a 3.23 can be used with a V8 with the same amount of success. The vehicle manufacturers offering trailer packages recommend specific axle ratios for each engine. These recommendations can be checked at your local dealer.

A small class in axle ratios is in order at this point. The axle ratio as pointed out above is based on the direct relationship between the turns of the driveshaft and the turning of the drive axles. Therefore, the higher the numerical ratio of the differential, the lower the gearing of the axle. An example is as follows. A differential with a ratio of 4.11 will cause the engine to turn faster to maintain a 50 mph speed than will an axle with a ratio of 3.23.

The object in choosing a rear axle is to combine the torque curve of the engine

with the appropriate ratio, keeping in mind the type of pulling which is to be done and formulating the correct ratio. As you can see this is a complicated task. Thankfully, the large car and truck manufacturers calculate the ratios and publish them in the trailer towing packages which are available when buying a new vehicle.

Concentrate on the correct ratio for towing; the harmful side effects are many at both extremes. If the ratio is too low (numerically), the clutch mechanism will slip more to get the unit moving, causing wear to the clutch mechanism. If the ratio is too high (numerically) the top speed of the rig is greatly lowered. The tendency with a very high differential ratio is to run the engine above the acceptable rpm range which will cause great damage to the engine. The importance of the correct ratio is thus evident.

WHEELS AND TIRES

Tire Selection

There are so many variables and possibilities when it comes to putting tires on your tow vehicle and trailer that it can become quite confusing.

Selecting tires for your tow vehicle is perhaps the more confusing of the two. What type of driving you will be doing? Over what kind of terrain? Will you be traveling at high speeds for long periods of time? Will you be traveling off the road

Camper trailer tire and wheel

very much? Will there be snow or mud where you're going? Will your tires be subjected to extremely high road temperatures?

There is a growing trend away from the conventional-bias tires to the bias-belted and radial plies. The conventional-bias tires are constructed so that the cord runs from one wire bead to the other, at an angle. Alternate plies run at an opposite angle. This type of construction gives rigidity to both the sidewall and the tread surface.

The construction of the radial tire differs from that of a conventional-bias tire in that the cords run from bead to bead at an approximate angle of 90 degrees. This construction gives the tread great rigidity and the sidewall great flexibility. The belts restrict the amount of "squirm" when the tread comes in contact with the pavement, thus improving tread life.

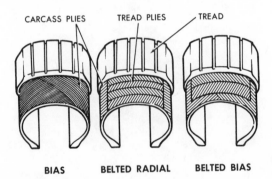

CARCASS PLIES   TREAD PLIES   TREAD

BIAS   BELTED RADIAL   BELTED BIAS

Construction of the bias, belted bias and the radial tire (© Chevrolet Div. G.M. Corp.)

The bias-belted tire is constructed in much the same manner as the conventional-bias tire. There are belts running at oblique and also at right angles to the bead as in the radial ply tire. This type of construction gives rigidity to the tread and sidewall of the tire. Tread life is improved over the conventional-bias tire but the objectional feeling of instability sometimes found in the flexible sidewalls of the radial is eliminated.

It is true that there is greater safety and longer tread life with tires of a higher load rating. These do, however, sacrifice the soft ride that original equipment tires provide.

WARNING: *Heavy-duty suspensions are a must for radial ply tires. Radial tires will "cup" and wear unevenly on a stan-dard, "mushy" suspension. Never mix radial-ply tires and any other type of tire on the same axle. If you decide to put wide flotation type tires on your tow vehicle, remember that they must not be installed on narrow rims. Extra-wide rims or wheels must be used.*

Tread design should be considered when selecting the tires for your tow vehicle. Decide what kind of driving you will be doing most frequently. Will you be driving off the road a lot? Will you be doing a lot of high-speed driving for long periods of time? A combination of both maybe, or strictly one or the other? For strictly off-road traveling, you'll want a heavy-duty tread design that will provide lots of traction and protect the tire against severe road conditions. For strictly highway use you would want a tread that will run quietly, deliver good mileage, and stay cool while running at high speeds. There are tires designed for both off-road on-road use which have a traction type tread design that stays relatively cool and quiet. Radials are not recommended for strictly off-road use because the stiff tread will cause the sidewalls to bulge when the tire meets an obstacle such as a rock. The sidewalls will bulge so much that they become susceptible to cuts and punctures.

Tire Pressure

Even pressure in the tow vehicle's tires plays an important part in the stability of the car-trailer unit. Low or uneven pressure can result in hard handling, erratic breaking, and possibly swerving—resulting in an accident. Overinflated tires tend to wear in the center and suffer a reduction in overall traction.

Do not trust a gas station tire pressure gauge. Surveys have shown some such gauges to be as inaccurate as 10 psi. Carry your own tire pressure gauge so each tire can be set correctly.

Wheels

The tire rim forms the direct union between the car and the tire. It absorbs the direct stress which the tires encounter and transfers it to the steering mechanism. Rims are usually maintenance-free and require little or no service. If a high-speed blowout (or any other accident where rim

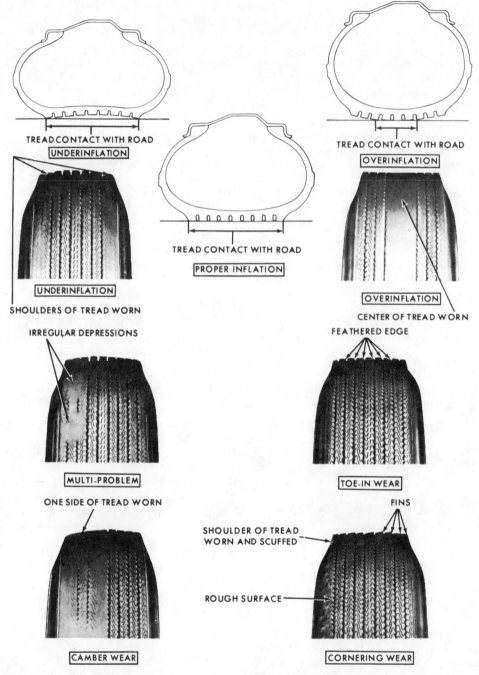

TREAD CONTACT WITH ROAD
UNDERINFLATION

TREAD CONTACT WITH ROAD
PROPER INFLATION

TREAD CONTACT WITH ROAD
OVERINFLATION

UNDERINFLATION
SHOULDERS OF TREAD WORN

OVERINFLATION
CENTER OF TREAD WORN

IRREGULAR DEPRESSIONS
MULTI-PROBLEM

FEATHERED EDGE
TOE-IN WEAR

ONE SIDE OF TREAD WORN
CAMBER WEAR

FINS
SHOULDER OF TREAD WORN AND SCUFFED
ROUGH SURFACE
CORNERING WEAR

Illustration showing abnormal tire wear patterns caused by improper inflation, misalignment, improper balance or suspension neglect.

damage is possible) occurs, the rims should be checked and replaced if found to be defective.

Have your tires mounted by a qualified mechanic who has the proper tools; damage to the wheel and the tire might otherwise result. Do not install larger tires on narrow rims. Oversized or wider rims should be used when increasing the tire size on your tow vehicle.

Passenger Car and Stationwagon Tire Load Limits

Load Range B (4-ply rating)
Load Range C (6-ply rating)
Load Range D (8-ply rating)

Bias 1965 On	Bias Pre 1965	Bias and Belted Bias 78 Series	70 Series	60 Series	Metric	Radial 78 Series	70 Series	20	22	24	26	28	30	32	34	36	38	40
6.00-13					165 R 13			770	820	860	900	930	970	1010	1040	1080	1110	1140
		A78-13	A70-13			AR 78-13	AR 70-13	810	860	900	940	980	1020	1060	1090	1130	1160	1200
6.50-13		B78-13	B70-13		175 R 13	BR 78-13	BR 70-13	890	930	980	1030	1070	1110	1150	1190	1230	1270	1300
		C78-13	C70-13			CR 78-13	CR 70-13	950	1000	1050	1100	1140	1190	1230	1270	1320	1360	1390
7.00-13					185 R 13			980	1030	1080	1130	1180	1230	1270	1310	1360	1400	1440
				D70-13		DR 78-13	DR 70-13	1010	1070	1120	1170	1220	1270	1320	1360	1410	1450	1490
				E70-13	195 R 13	ER 78-13	ER 70-13	1060	1110	1170	1220	1280	1320	1370	1440	1490	1540	1580
								1070	1130	1190	1240	1300	1350	1400				
				A70-14	155 R 14		AR 70-14	780	820	860	900	940	970	1010	1090	1130	1160	1200
								810	860	900	940	980	1020	1060				
6.45-14	6.00-14	B78-14	B70-14		165 R 14	BR 78-14	BR 70-14	860	910	960	1000	1040	1080	1120	1160	1200	1240	1270
								840	900	930	980	1020	1060	1100	1130	1170	1210	1240
								890	930	980	1030	1070	1110	1150	1190	1230	1270	1300
6.95-14	6.50-14	C78-14	C70-14		175 R 14	CR 78-14	CR 70-14	950	1000	1050	1100	1140	1190	1230	1270	1310	1350	1390
								950	1000	1050	1100	1140	1190	1230	1270	1320	1360	1400
								930	990	1030	1080	1130	1170	1210	1250	1300	1330	1370
		D78-14	D70-14			DR 78-14	DR 70-14	1010	1070	1120	1170	1220	1270	1320	1360	1410	1450	1490

TIRE SIZE OR DESIGNATION — Cold Inflation Pressures—Pounds Per Square Inch

17

Passenger Car and Stationwagon Tire Load Limits (cont.)

Load Range B (4-ply rating)
Load Range C (6-ply rating)
Load Range D (8-ply rating)

Bias		Bias and Belted Bias		60 Series	Metric	Radial		Cold Inflation Pressures—Pounds Per Square Inch										
1965 On	Pre 1965	78 Series	70 Series			78 Series	70 Series	20	22	24	26	28	30	32	34	36	38	40
7.35-14	7.00-14	E78-14	E70-14		185 R 14	ER 78-14	ER 70-14	1040	1100	1160	1210	1260	1310	1360	1400	1450	1490	1540
								1030	1100	1140	1190	1240	1290	1340	1380	1430	1470	1520
								1070	1130	1190	1240	1300	1350	1400	1440	1490	1540	1580
7.75-14	7.50-14	F78-14	F70-14		195 R 14	FR 78-14	FR 70-14	1150	1210	1270	1330	1390	1440	1500	1550	1600	1650	1690
								1150	1230	1280	1340	1390	1450	1500	1550	1600	1650	1700
								1160	1220	1280	1340	1400	1450	1500	1550	1610	1650	1700
8.25-14	8.00-14	G78-14	G70-14		205 R 14	GR 78-14	GR 70-14	1250	1310	1380	1440	1500	1560	1620	1670	1730	1780	1830
								1240	1320	1380	1440	1500	1560	1620	1670	1730	1780	1830
								1250	1310	1380	1440	1500	1560	1620	1680	1730	1780	1830
8.55-14	8.50-14	H78-14	H70-14		215 R 14	HR 78-14	HR 70-14	1360	1430	1510	1580	1640	1710	1770	1830	1890	1950	2000
								1330	1420	1480	1550	1610	1670	1740	1790	1850	1910	1960
								1360	1440	1510	1580	1650	1710	1770	1830	1890	1950	2010
8.85-14	9.00-14	J78-14	J70-14		225 R 14	JR 78-14	JR 70-14	1430	1510	1580	1660	1730	1790	1860	1920	1990	2050	2100
								1430	1500	1580	1650	1720	1790	1860	1920	1980	2040	2100
			K70-14				KR 70-14	1460	1540	1620	1690	1770	1830	1900	1970	2030	2090	2150
9.50-14			L70-14				LR 70-14	1540	1640	1700	1780	1850	1930	2000	2060	2130	2200	2260
								1520	1600	1680	1750	1830	1900	1970	2040	2100	2170	2230
6.00-15					165 R 15	BR 78-15		870	910	960	1000	1050	1090	1130				
								890	930	980	1030	1070	1110	1150	1190	1230	1270	1300
								890	940	980	1030	1070	1110	1150				
6.85-15	6.50-15	C78-15	C70-15		175 R 15	CR 78-15	CR 70-15	950	1000	1050	1100	1140	1190	1230	1270	1320	1360	1390
								950	1000	1050	1100	1140	1190	1230	1270	1320	1360	1400
								980	1040	1080	1130	1180	1230	1270	1320	1360	1400	1440

Tire sizes	1490	1450	1410	1360	1320	1270	1220	1170	1120	1070	1010
7.35-15 / D78-15 / D70-15 / DR 78-15 / DR 70-15 / 185 R 15 / E60-15	1570	1530	1480	1440	1390	1340	1290	1240	1180	1130	1070
	1580	1540	1490	1440	1400	1350	1300	1240	1190	1130	1070
7.75-15 / E78-15 / E70-15 / ER 78-15 / ER 70-15 / 195 R 15 / F60-15	1690	1640	1590	1540	1490	1440	1380	1330	1270	1210	1150
6.70-15	1640	1590	1550	1500	1450	1400	1340	1290	1230	1190	1110
	1700	1650	1610	1550	1500	1450	1400	1340	1280	1220	1160
7.10-15 / F78-15 / F70-15 / FR 78-15 / FR 70-15 / 205 R 15 / G60-15	1820	1770	1720	1660	1610	1550	1490	1430	1370	1300	1240
	1760	1710	1660	1600	1550	1500	1440	1380	1320	1270	1190
8.25-15 / G78-15 / G70-15 / GR 78-15 / GR 70-15	1830	1780	1730	1680	1620	1560	1500	1440	1380	1310	1250
	1830	1780	1730	1670	1620	1560	1500	1440	1380	1310	1250
7.60-15 / H78-15 / H70-15 / HR 78-15 / HR 70-15 / 215 R 15	1970	1920	1860	1800	1740	1680	1620	1550	1480	1410	1340
	1930	1880	1820	1760	1710	1640	1580	1520	1450	1400	1310
8.55-15	2010	1950	1890	1830	1770	1710	1650	1580	1510	1440	1360
	2000	1950	1890	1830	1770	1710	1640	1580	1510	1430	1360
8.85-15 / J78-15 / J70-15 / JR 78-15 / JR 70-15 / 225 R 15	2100	2040	1980	1920	1860	1790	1720	1650	1580	1510	1430
8.00-15	2040	1980	1920	1860	1800	1730	1670	1600	1530	1470	1380
	2100	2040	1980	1920	1860	1790	1720	1650	1580	1500	1430
9.00-15 / K70-15 / KR 70-15	2150	2090	2030	1970	1900	1830	1760	1690	1620	1540	1460
8.20-15	2170	2110	2050	1980	1920	1850	1780	1710	1630	1570	1470
	2150	2090	2030	1970	1900	1830	1770	1690	1620	1540	1460
9.15-15 / L78-15 / L70-15 / LR 78-15 / LR 70-15 / 235 R 15	2230	2160	2100	2030	1970	1900	1830	1750	1680	1600	1510
	2230	2170	2100	2040	1970	1900	1830	1750	1680	1600	1520
M78-15	2370	2300	2230	2160	2090	2020	1940	1860	1780	1700	1610
8.90-15 / N78-15	2500	2430	2360	2280	2210	2130	2050	1970	1880	1790	1700
	2500	2430	2360	2290	2210	2130	2050	1970	1880	1810	1700
6.00-16			1500	1450	1400	1350	1300	1250	1195	1135	1075

Passenger Car and Stationwagon Tire Load Limits (cont.)

Load Range B (4-ply rating)
Load Range C (6-ply rating)
Load Range D (8-ply rating)

TIRE SIZE OR DESIGNATION								Cold Inflation Pressures—Pounds Per Square Inch										
Bias		Bias and Belted Bias			Metric	Radial		20	22	24	26	28	30	32	34	36	38	40
1965 On	Pre 1965	78 Series	70 Series	60 Series		78 Series	70 Series											
6.50-16								1215	1280	1345	1405	1465	1525	1580	1635	1690		
7.00-15								1310	1380	1450	1515	1580	1640	1700	1760	1820		
7.00-16								1365	1440	1515	1585	1650	1715	1780	1840	1900		

NOTES:

1. Ply Rating   While there is no industry-wide definition of ply rating, passenger car tires marked "4-ply rating/2-ply" have the same load carrying capacity as a current or most recent 4-ply tire of the same size at the same inflation. Passenger car tires marked "8-ply rating/4-ply" have the same load carrying capacity as 8-ply rating tires of the same size at the same inflation, regardless of the actual number of plies.

2. Load Range   The "load range" system is now being used in tire marketing with letters (e.g., Load Range B, C, D, etc.) to identify tires with their particular load and inflation limits and service requirements. While the ply rating system is being gradually phased out, both designations may be used on tire sidewalls and are shown in the tables above. During their interim period Load Range B tires may be marked 4-ply rating/2-ply or 4-ply; Load Range C tires, 6-ply rating/4-ply or 6-ply and Load Range D tires, 8-ply rating/4-ply, 8-ply rating/6-ply or 8-ply.

20

Trailer Tire Load Ratings

Size	Load Range	Ply Rating	Load Limits (lbs per tire) at Various Cold Inflation Pressures														
			30	35	40	45	50	55	60	65	70	75	80	85	90	95	100
6.00-16 LT	C	6	1130	1230	1330	1430											
6.50-16 LT	C	6	1270	1390	1500	1610											
6.70-15 LT	C	6	1210	1320	1430	1530											
7.00-13 LT	C	6	1000	1090	1170	1260											
7.00-13 LT	D	8	1000	1090	1170	1260	1340	1420	1490								
7.00-14 LT	C	6	1030	1130	1220	1310											
7.00-14 LT	D	8	1030	1130	1220	1310	1390	1470	1550								
7.00-14 LT	E	10	1030	1130	1220	1310	1390	1470	1550								
7.00-15 LT	C	6	1350	1480	1610	1720											
7.00-15 LT	D	8	1350	1480	1610	1720	1830	1940	2040								
7.00-16 LT	C	6	1430	1560	1680	1800											
7.00-16 LT	D	8	1430	1560	1680	1880	1910	2030	2130								
7.10-15 LT	C	6	1320	1440	1560	1670											
7.50-15 LT	D	8	1560	1710	1840	1980	2100	2220	2330								
7.50-15 LT	E	10	1560	1710	1840	1980	2100	2220	2330	2450	2560	2660					
7.50-16 LT	C	6	1620	1770	1930	2060											
7.50-16 LT	D	8	1620	1770	1930	2060	2190	2310	2440								
7.50-16 LT	E	10	1620	1770	1930	2060	2190	2310	2440	2560	2670	2780					
8.25-16 LT	D	8	1980	2160	2330	2500	2660	2820									
8.25-16 LT	E	10	1980	2160	2330	2500	2660	2820	2960								
9.00-16 LT	D	8	2250	2460	2660	2850	3030										
9.00-16 LT	E	10	2250	2460	2660	2850	3030	3210	3370								
7-14.5	D	8	1140	1240	1350	1440	1530	1620	1710	1790	1870						
7-14.5	E	10	1140	1240	1350	1440	1530	1620	1710	1790	1870	1940	2020	2090			
7-14.5	F	12	1140	1240	1350	1440	1530	1620	1710	1790	1870	1940	2020	2090	2160	2230	2300
8-14.5	E	10	1380	1510	1630	1750	1860	1970	2070	2170	2270	2360	2450	2540			
8-14.5	F	12	1380	1510	1630	1750	1860	1970	2070	2170	2270	2360	2450	2540	2620	2710	2790

Conventional Truck Tire Load Ratings

Size	Load Range	Ply Rating	Load Limits (lbs per tire) at Various Cold Inflation Pressures																
			20	25	30	35	40	45	50	55	60	65	70	75	80	85	90	95	100
4.10-6	B	4	185	210	235	260	280	300	320	335	350	370							
4.80-8	A	2	305	345	385	425	455	490	520	550	580	610							
4.80-8	B	4	305	345	385	425	455	490	520	550	580	610							
4.80-8	C	6	305	345	385	425	455	490	520	550	580	610	635	660	685	710	735		
4.80-9	A	2	330	375	415														
4.80-9	B	4	330	375	415	455	495	530	560	595	625	655							
4.80-12	B	4	405	465	515	565	610	655	695	735	775	810							
4.80-12	C	6	405	465	515	565	610	655	695	735	775	810	845	880	915	950	980		
5.30-6	A	2	310	355	395	430	465	500	530	560									
5.30-6	B	4	310	355	395	430	465	500	530	560									
5.30-12	B	4	485	550	615	670	725	780	825	875									
5.70-8	B	4	420	480	535	585	630	675	720	760	800	835							
5.70-8	C	6	420	480	535	585	630	675	720	760	800	835	875	910					
5.70-8	D	8	420	480	535	585	630	675	720	760	800	835	875	910					
6.50-10	C	6	685	775	865	945	1020	1100	1170	1230	1300								
6.50-10	E	10	685	775	865	945	1020	1100	1170	1230	1300	1360	1420	1480	1540	1590	1650	1700	1759
6.90-9	B	4	580	655	730	800	865	925	985	1045	1095								
6.90-9	C	6	580	655	730	800	865	925	985	1045	1095								
6.90-9	E	10	580	655	730	800	865	925	985	1045	1095	1150	1200	1250	1300	1345	1400	1435	1480
6.90-12	B	4	690	785	875	955	1035	1105	1175	1245	1310								
6.90-12	C	6	690	785	875	955	1035	1105	1175	1245	1310								
7.00-10	D	8	765	870	970	1060	1140	1230	1300	1380	1450	1520	1590						
7.00-10	E	10	765	870	970	1060	1140	1230	1300	1390	1450	1520	1590	1650	1720	1780			
7.50-10	E	10	825	935	1040	1140	1230	1320	1400	1490	1560	1640	1710	1780					
9.00-10	E	10	1110	1260	1400	1530	1650	1770	1890	2000	2100	2200							

Size	Range	Ply														
6.50-13 ST	B	4	705	800	895	980	1060	1130	1200	1275						
6.50-13 ST	C	6	705	800	895	980	1060	1130	1200	1275						
7.75-14 ST	B	4	895	1020	1140	1240	1340	1440	1530							
7.75-14 ST	C	6	895	1020	1140	1240	1340	1440	1530							
7.75-15 ST	B	4	895	1020	1140	1240	1340	1440	1530							
7.75-15 ST	C	6	895	1020	1140	1240	1340	1440	1530							
16.5 x 6.5-8	A	2	415	475	525	570	615									
16.5 x 6.5-8	B	4	415	475	525	570	615	695	735							
16.5 x 6.5-8	C	6	415	475	525	570	615	695	735	770						
20.5 x 8.0-10	B	4	655	745	820	895	965	1030	1090							
20.5 x 8.0-10	C	6	655	745	820	895	965	1030	1090	1150						
20.5 x 8.0-10	D	8	655	745	820	895	965	1030	1090	1150	1210	1270	1320			
20.5 x 8.0-10	E	10	655	745	820	895	965	1030	1090	1150	1210	1270	1320	1370	1420	1470
18.5 x 8.5-8	B	4	560	630	700	760	820	875	930							
18.5 x 8.5-8	C	6	560	630	700	760	820	875	930							
23.5 x 8.5-12	B	4	805	910	1010	1100	1180	1260	1340							
23.5 x 8.5-12	C	6	805	910	1010	1100	1180	1260	1340							

High-Flotation Truck Tire Load Ratings

Size	Load Range	Ply Rating	Maximum Tire Loads (pounds) at Various Cold Inflation Pressures (psi)												
			30	35	40	45	50	55	60	65	70	75	80	85	90
8.00-16.5	B	4	1360												
8.00-16.5	C	6	1360	1490	1610	1730									
8.00-16.5	D	8	1360	1490	1610	1730	1840	1945	2045						
8.00-16.5	E	10	1360	1490	1610	1730	1840	1945	2045	2145	2240	2330			
8.00-16.5	F	12	1360	1490	1610	1730	1840	1945	2045	2145	2240	2330	2420	2500	2590
8.75-16.5	B	4	1570												
8.75-16.5	C	6	1570	1720	1850	1990									
8.75-16.5	D	8	1570	1720	1850	1990	2110	2240	2350						
8.75-16.5	E	10	1570	1720	1850	1990	2110	2240	2350	2470	2570	2680			
9.50-16.5	B	4	1860												
9.50-16.5	C	6	1860	2030	2190	2350									
9.50-16.5	D	8	1860	2030	2190	2350	2500	2650	2780						
9.50-16.5	E	10	1860	2030	2190	2350	2500	2650	2780	2920	3050	3170			
10-16.5	B	4	1840												
10-16.5	C	6	1840	2010	2170	2330									
10-16.5	D	8	1840	2010	2170	2330	2480	2620	2750						
10-17.5	C	6	1910	2095	2265	2425									
10-17.5	D	8	1910	2095	2265	2425	2580	2730	2870						
10-17.5	E	10	1910	2095	2265	2425	2580	2730	2870	3010	3140	3270			
10-17.5	F	12	1910	2095	2265	2425	2580	2730	2870	3010	3140	3270	3395	3520	3640
12-16.5	D	8	2370	2590	2800	3000									
12-16.5	E	10	2370	2590	2800	3000	3190	3370	3550						
14-17.5	C	6	3210												
14-17.5	D	8	3210	3500	3790	4060									
14-17.5	E	10	3210	3500	3790	4060	4320	4570	4800						
14-17.5	F	12	3210	3500	3790	4060	4320	4570	4800	5030	5260	5470			
14-17.5	G	14	3210	3500	3790	4060	4320	4570	4800	5030	5260	5470	5680	5890	6090
10-15	B	4	1760												
10-15	C	6	1760	1930	2080	2230									
10-15	D	8	1760	1930	2080	2230	2370	2510	2640						
10-16	B	4	1840												
10-16	C	6	1840	2010	2170	2330									
10-16	D	8	1840	2010	2170	2330	2480	2620	2750						
11-14	B	4	1820												
11-14	C	6	1820	1990	2150	2300									
11-14	D	8	1820	1990	2150	2300	2450	2590	2730						
11-15	B	4	1900												
11-15	C	6	1900	2080	2250	2410									
11-15	D	8	1900	2080	2250	2410	2560	2710	2850						
11-16	B	4	1980												
11-16	C	6	1980	2160	2330	2500									
11-16	D	8	1980	2160	2330	2500	2650	2810	2950						

NOTE: For the tire sizes not listed, consult your tire supplier, or write Rubber Manufacturer's Assoc. for load and inflation information.

AIR SHOCK ABSORBERS

Air shocks are a relatively new addition to the camping field. These are conventional shock absorbers with internal power pistons which expand and contract when air pressure is applied. They were first used in racing when the car's suspension had to be raised or lowered to compensate for varying track conditions.

These shock absorbers can be a welcome solution to the rear-end sag problem of tow cars. Since camper trailers have relatively low hitch height, the installation of an air shock assembly—with no other suspension changes—can regain the normal riding height of the car.

Installation is relatively simple. Merely replace the conventional shock absorbers, using the same mounting brackets. The only addition necessary is the placement of the air line (used to fill the shocks) which is usually mounted in the trunk. With the hitch in place, the shocks can be filled to the proper level so the car is horizontal. With the trailer removed, they can be deflated to give the car a smoother, even ride. (See the tow vehicle section for illustrations.)

Check with your trailer dealer regarding the correct shocks for your needs and the correct procedures for installation and use.

DEALER TRAILER PACKAGES

Since more and more towing is done with conventional automobiles, manufacturers now offer cars with the necessary heavy-duty equipment to meet the added requirements. Such drive train components as heavy-duty batteries, transmissions, cooling and electrical systems, suspensions, and engines are provided in an optional package to prepare a car for trailer towing.

Your dealer can show you a special brochure which will present an orderly arrangement of the packages available with each model of car. The charts in this book will provide most of the same information.

4-WHEEL-DRIVE

Four-wheel-drive (4wd) vehicles have recently gained great popularity in the recreational field. The idea started with individuals who bought surplus jeeps and discovered a new form of recreation in off-road driving. Manufacturers gradually entered the 4wd market and have ex-

Four wheel drive Blazer with Nimrod trailer (© Chevrolet Div. G.M. Corp.)

panded their lines to currently offer a wide variety of these vehicles.

A 4wd vehicle is basically the same as a conventional, two-wheel rear-drive model but it has been combined with a front-drive axle with a power drive to pull while the rear-drive axle pushes. The addition of a front-drive axle doubles traction.

Driving early 4wd models was anything but comfortable since the front axle was always engaged and the front suspension was rigid. Today, however, this is all changed. The front differential can be disengaged while the vehicle is on smooth pavement and then engaged when off-road traction is necessary. The suspensions have also been modified so comfort does not suffer excessively.

Since traction is the key word when towing, a 4wd vehicle can make an excellent tow vehicle. This is not to suggest an immediate purchase on these merits, but it should be considered if you intend to do a great deal of off-road camping. Your local dealer can explain which vehicles offer a 4wd option and can explain the different components.

TOW HITCHES

Hitches have only two basic components: the tow bar and the coupler. The tow bar is fastened to the car (either frame or bumper). The coupler contains the hitch ball and connects to the tongue of the trailer.

There are three basic types of hitch: frame-mounted; axle-mounted; and the equalizing type hitch. These will be discussed further under their own headings.

Any of these hitches should be strong, but with a reasonably heavy trailer, it is especially critical. A custom hitch is rarely necessary with camper trailers, but may become so as the tongue weight increases.

All well-mounted hitches should be fastened at three points on the tow vehicle body because a three-point attachment offers the required stability and strength. If you are a novice, consult a qualified hitch dealer before buying any hitch. This is an important piece of equipment, with an expensive car in front and an expensive trailer behind it, and it won't take long for trouble to develop if you weren't careful in selecting the proper hitch.

Frame and Axle Tow Hitches

Frame hitches are the least expensive to buy. They are usually made of a straight or slightly off-set beam which is attached to the frame and also to the rear bumper. The trailer hitch ball, which engages the coupler of the trailer, is on the other end of the support beam. This type of hitch is generally not used with any type of trailer above 2000 lbs gross vehicle weight and a tongue weight over 200 lbs.

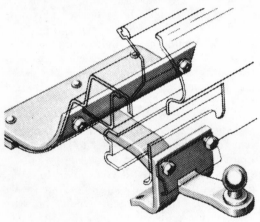

Non-equalizing hitch

The axle hitch is fastened on either side of the axle housing with two support rods which intersect and are fastened at the rear bumper. The axle support hitch centers the pulling power of the car on the stable rear axle housing.

This type of hitch is not recommended for towing modern heavier trailers such as

travel trailers. Even though the hitch is fastened to the tow vehicle's bumper or frame at the very rear of the car, there is a certain amount of forward-backward flexing and strain put on the axle housing where the other end of the hitch is fastened. A certain amount of this flexing is present with all hitches even if they are properly installed. On others than the axle hitch, the flexing occurs at points where the least amount of harm is done (e.g., frame and bumper). With the axle hitch, however, the flexing is present on the rear axle housing of the tow vehicle and can cause bent or cracked axle housings, bent or broken U-bolts that attach the axles to the leaf springs, and (on cars with rear coil springs) damage to upper and lower control arms.

Trailer Equalizing Hitches

The object of a trailer-equalizing hitch is to keep the tow car in a reasonably level condition despite the additional tongue weight of the rear of the car. The physics of this hitch distributes the hitch weight of the trailer between the front and rear wheels of the car and the trailer wheels.

It is easy to see in the following example. A 200 lb weight in the trunk of a conventional auto causes the rear of the vehicle to slope down. If we weld two five-foot pieces of metal beam a foot equidistant from the center of the rear bumper, a man can raise the car to its original height by simply lifting.

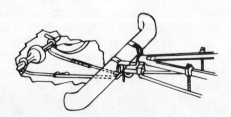

Axle type hitch

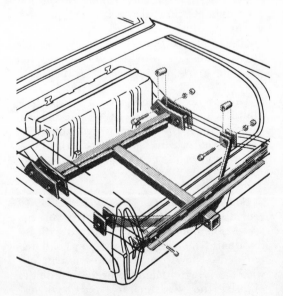

Load equalizing hitch

Substituting a camper trailer with a hitch of 200 lbs for the weight in the trunk will again cause the car to slope to the rear. But again, a man can restore the car to level by exerting the same upward pressure on the two beams. Suppose we fasten the beam supports to the trailer tongue with chains while the man is lifting. Now the manual pressure can be released and neither the car nor the trailer moves down. What has happened? The weight has distributed itself. One-third has been placed on the front wheels of the car while one-third has been placed on the rear wheels of the car. The remaining third is positioned on the wheels of the trailer. This is how a weight distribution hitch works. As you can see, when this hitch is connected properly, both trailer and car should be level.

The solid beams extending from the tow vehicle are usually made of spring steel to flex when severe vertical pressure is applied to them as might happen if the tow vehicle hits a deep hole.

INSTALLATION OF A TRAILER HITCH

Installing a trailer hitch is no job for a novice, if the trailer is fairly large (Class II, III). Class I hitches can be installed by almost anyone with common hand tools. An experienced, competent trailer service center with trained mechanics should install the hitch. This is also no place for penny pinching. The difference in cost between a corner-cutting installation and one done correctly should not be more than a few dollars. This is not to say that you shouldn't shop around to get the best price on a hitch installation. You must simply put the emphasis on quality and not on price.

There are a lot of companies that design and make prefab trailer hitches for each make of car. These can be trusted to be strong enough if the hitch is installed correctly and you do not tow anything heavier than is recommended by the manufacturer.

If you have to have a hitch custom made, inspect the material that the hitch is to be made from. Check to be sure the steel is a heavy enough gauge, and strong enough to carry the load of your trailer. Remember to look for quality—not the lowest price. Check among your friends to find shops that install trailer hitches and have a reputation for good work. Maybe you would like to visit a few of the shops you had in mind and look them over. A certain amount of equipment is essential for installing and fabricating hitches. Metal-bending and cutting tools, welders, hoists, power-impact wrenches, and jack-stands to hold parts into place for cutting and fitting should be readily visible. Check over some of the installer's work. You don't have to be an expert to be able to see poor workmanship which indicates indifference. Examine the welds carefully to see if the beads are of even width; they should look like a line of evenly spaced crescent shapes. Pockmarks, large lumps of burnt material, or otherwise interrupted beads are a sign of poor welding.

The frame of the tow vehicle might require reinforcement before the hitch is installed. This is particularly true of cars with the unit body frame construction. An experienced hitch installer can tell if the frame on your car needs extra reinforcement.

There seems to be a bit of discrepancy about how a trailer hitch should be attached to a tow vehicle. Some people say to bolt it on and others say to weld it. All we can do is give the advantages and disadvantages of both.

The advantages of having the hitch welded are:

1. Gives a better bond to the frame of the tow vehicle;
2. Spreads the load over a wider area;
3. Will not work loose as bolts might.

Disadvantages:

1. Welded job is only as good as the welder;
2. Welds can break without warning;
3. Heat created by welding could warp or distort the frame of the tow vehicle and could even change the properties of the metal, making it softer or more brittle.

The advantages of having the hitch bolted on are:

1. Squeaks and rattles will let you know if the bolts do work loose;
2. Bolted-on hitches are easier to remove for switching over to another vehicle or to store for the winter;
3. Easier to install.

Disadvantages:

1. Bolts can work loose;
2. Some car manufacturers recommend that holes not be drilled in the frame of the car;

3. Should a bolt fall out, it cannot be replaced with an average bolt, instead they must be made of a harder grade of steel;

4. Stress is placed on one small area, right where the bolt is placed through the frame.

Check to see that the height of the hitch ball is the same as the height of the coupler on your trailer when it is level. Also allow at least ¼ in. gap between the gas tank and the floor of the car and all bars and brackets of the installed hitches. Friction from vibration could wear a hole.

Most people seem to think that installation procedures are all the attention a hitch needs. Not so. To give years of dependable service, the hitch should be properly maintained. Here are a few pointers on hitch maintenance.

1. Keep the hitch ball tight. Never install a hitch ball without the correct lockwasher and shank nut.

2. Keep all of the nuts and bolts that attach the hitch to the car tight.

3. Lubricate the ball occasionally with light lubricant; heavy grease will attract and hold abrasives that could do more damage than the grease could help.

4. Check all levers, pins, and working joints for signs of wear. Lubricate them with a light lubricant and replace them if they show signs of extreme wear and/or the possibility of breakage.

5. Spray the hitch and tongue of the trailer with a rust-inhibiting paint from time to time. This should help to retard corrosion and extend useful hitch life.

6. Examine the safety chains regularly. Chains sometimes drag on the ground and wear to a point of possible failure if the trailer becomes disconnected from the tow vehicle. Replace the chains if they are worn to a point that you think unsafe.

BRAKES

The tow vehicle serves as the major portion of the braking system of the car-trailer unit. Optional tow equipment packages consider this and choose either heavy-duty shoe brakes or disc brakes.

Although heavy-duty shoe brakes offer maximum stopping power, disc brakes are worth the extra money. Their resistance to fade and the excess build-up of heat which causes brake failure is an asset which cannot be overlooked.

If the vehicle is not equipped with a

A disc brake

towing package, the stock factory equipment brake linings can be replaced with center metallic bonded linings. These are harder than the factory linings and will increase the braking power of the car greatly—especially when the brakes are warm.

FLEXIBLE FANS

A frequent hazard of towing a trailer is the tendency for the cooling system to overload and overheat. This generally happens with cars which are not equipped with trailer towing packages. To alleviate this problem, either a larger fan or fan shrouding, or a combination of both, are in order. A few companies (the best known is Flex-a-lite®) presently produce light-weight fiberglass fans for recreational vehicles. The idea was first initiated in racing cars; maximum cooling was needed at low engine rpm with a limited amount of component weight.

The fan is composed of a fiberglass-reinforced material which is relatively pliable. This construction produces a unit which is light in weight (approximately ¼ of the weight of the stock unit) and produces twice the cooling capacity at low speed.

The fan works in the following manner: at the idle speed or low engine rpm the blades of the fan are at a severe angle, cutting the air at a greater degree and causing a great amount of air to be sucked through the radiator. As the engine speed increases, the centrifugal force of the fan turning at greater speed causes the blades

A flex-type fan

clutch type fans for engine cooling. These have a heat-sensing mechanism built into the center shaft of the fan itself. If the engine is relatively cold, the mechanism will allow the fan to "free wheel" until the sensor's heat mechanism reacts to the running temperature. At running temperatures, the clutch engages inside the fan and the fan turns again at a one-to-one ratio with the fan shaft.

to bend, thus decreasing the angle of the blades and the amount of air being moved. This lowering of the fan's function is desirable because more air is channeled through the radiator without the help of the fan as the vehicle's forward speed increases. Another advantage of the flexible fan is that, unlike fans with large blades, it makes only a limited amount of noise—even at high rpm.

CLUTCHING FANS

Newer models with either trailer packages or air conditioning are equipped with

Clutch fan

Trailer Towing Recommendations

Note: Up to 2000 LBS—Class I (Light)   N.A.—Not Available
2000–3500 LBS—Class II (Medium)   ——Not Applicable
3500–5000 LBS—Class III (Heavy)   Std.—Standard
                                          H.D.—Heavy Duty

UNDER NO CIRCUMSTANCES SHOULD A FRAME TYPE HITCH BE INSTALLED ON A 1973 COLLAPSIBLE BUMPER.

1972 Trailer Towing Information

Matador & Ambassador

Equipment	Class I	Class II	Class III
Trailer Type	Any	Any	Any
Tongue Load Limit (lbs)	250	350	500
Engine Requirement	360 cu in., 2 bbl.	360 cu in., 2 bbl.	360 cu in., 2 bbl.
Exhaust System	Std.	Std.	Std.
Engine Cooling	Std.	H.D.	H.D.
Transmission Requirement	"Torque-Command" Automatic	"Torque-Command" Automatic	"Torque-Command" Automatic
Trans. Aux. Oil Cooler	——	Required	Required
Axle Ratio Recommended	Std.	Highest-Numerical Ratio for particular Engine/ Transmission combination	Highest-Numerical Ratio for particular Engine/ Transmission combination
Differential Type	Std.	"Twin-Grip"	"Twin-Grip"
Wheels Recommended	Std.	Std.	Std.
Tires	Next size option for particular Model/Engine combination		
Brakes Recommended	Power	Power	Power
Front	Drum or Disc	Drum or Disc	Drum or Disc
Rear	Drum	Drum	Drum
Springs	H.D.②	H.D.②	H.D.②
Shock Absorbers	H.D.②	Air shocks②	Air Shocks②
Sway Bar	——	——	——
Steering Recommended	Power	Power	Power
Battery Recommended	Std.	70 Amp	70 Amp

1972 Trailer Towing Information (cont.)

Matador & Ambassador

Equipment	Class I	Class II	Class III
Alternator	Std.	Std.	Std.
Turn Signal Flasher	Std.	Std.	Std.
Type Hitch Required①	Body Mounted or Equalizer	Equalizer	Equalizer

① Not available as factory options.
② H.D.—Heavy Duty American Motors

1972 Trailer Towing Information

Gremlin & Hornet

Equipment	Class I	Class II	Class III
Trailer Type	Low Silhouette①	——	——
Tongue Load Limit (lbs)	Up to 150	——	——
Engine Requirement	Any	——	——
Exhaust System	Std.	——	——
Engine Cooling	Std.	——	——
Transmission Requirement	Any	——	——
Trans. Aux. Oil Cooler	——	——	——
Axle Ratio Recommended	Std.②	——	——
Differential Type	Std.	——	——
Wheels Recommended	Std.	——	——
Tires	Std.	——	——
Brakes Recommended	Std.	——	——
Front	——	——	——
Rear	——	——	——
Springs	Std.	——	——
Shock Absorbers	Std.	——	——
Sway Bar	——	——	——

1972 Trailer Towing Information (cont.)

Gremlin & Hornet

Equipment	Class I	Class II	Class III
Steering Recommended	Std.	——	——
Battery Recommended	Std.	——	——
Alternator	Std.	——	——
Turn Signal Flasher	Std.	——	——
Type Hitch Required③	Body Mounted or Equalizer	——	——

① Low Silhouette—defined as level with car top height.
② Recommended minimum of 2.73:1 ratio with 232 cu in. engine.
③ Not available as factory options.

1968–'69 Trailer Towing Information

American Motors

Equipment	Class I	Class II	Class III
Trailer Type	Any	Any	Any
Tongue Load Limit (lbs)	250	350	500
Engine Requirement	232 cu in. Six	290 cu in. V-8	343 cu in. V-8
Exhaust System	Std.	Std.	Std.
Engine Cooling	H.D.	H.D.	H.D.
Transmission Requirement	Shift Command Automatic		
Trans. Aux. Oil Cooler	Required	Required	Required
Axle Ratio Recommended	3.15:1①	3.15:1	3.15:1
Differential Type	Twin-Grip	Twin-Grip	Twin-Grip
Wheels Recommended	Std.	Std.	Std.
Tires	Std.	Std.	Std. size 8 Ply rated Extra size 4 Ply rated
Brakes Recommended	Power	Power	Power
Front	——	——	——
Rear	——	——	——

1968–'69 Trailer Towing Information (cont.)

American Motors

Equipment	Class I	Class II	Class III
Springs	H.D.②	H.D.②	H.D.②
Shock Absorbers	H.D.②	H.D.②	H.D.②
Sway Bar	——	——	——
Steering Recommended	Power	Power	Power
Battery Recommended	Std.	Std.	Std.
Alternator	Std.	Std.	Std.
Turn Signal Flasher	Std.	Std.	Std.
Type Hitch Required	Body Mounted	Equalizer	Equalizer

① 3.31:1 ratio with six cylinder
② American Motors Handling Package

1971 Trailer Towing Information

Matador & Ambassador

Equipment	Class I	Class II	Class III
Trailer Type	Any	Any	Any
Tongue Load Limit (lbs)	250	350	500
Engine Requirement	232 cu in. Six	304 cu in. V-8	360 cu in. V-8
Exhaust System	Std.	Std.	Std.
Engine Cooling	H.D.	H.D.	H.D.
Transmission Requirement	Shift Command Automatic		
Trans. Aux. Oil Cooler	Required	Std.	Std.
Axle Ratio Recommended	Highest numerical ratio for particular Engine/Transmission combination		
Differential Type	Twin-Grip	Twin-Grip	Twin-Grip
Wheels Recommended	Std.	Std.	Std.
Tires	Largest size option for particular Model/Engine combination		

1971 Trailer Towing Information (cont.)

Matador & Ambassador

Equipment	Class I	Class II	Class III
Brakes Recommended	Power	Power	Power
Front	Drums or Disc	Drums or Disc	Drums or Disc
Rear	Drums	Drums	Drums
Springs	H.D.①	H.D.①	H.D.①
Shock Absorbers	H.D.①	H.D.①	Air shocks
Sway Bar	——	——	——
Steering Recommended	Power	Power	Power
Battery Recommended	H.D.	H.D.	H.D.
Alternator	H.D.	H.D.	H.D.
Turn Signal Flasher	H.D.	H.D.	H.D.
Type Hitch Required	Body Mounted	Equalizer	Equalizer

① American Motors Handling Package

1971 Trailer Towing Information

Gremlin & Hornet

Equipment	Class I	Class II	Class III
Trailer Type	Up to 1000 lbs	——	——
Tongue Load Limit (lbs)	Up to 150	——	——
Engine Requirement	Any	——	——
Exhaust System	Std.	——	——
Engine Cooling	Std.	——	——
Transmission Requirement	Any	——	——
Trans. Aux. Oil Cooler Std. V-8s Opt 6s	Required	——	——
Axle Ratio Recommended	Std.	——	——
Differential Type	Std.	——	——
Wheels Recommended	Std.	——	——

1971 Trailer Towing Information (cont.)

Gremlin & Hornet

Equipment	Class I	Class II	Class III
Tires	Std.	——	——
Brakes Recommended	Std.	——	——
Front	Std.	——	——
Rear	Std.	——	——
Springs	Std.	——	——
Shock Absorbers	Std.	——	——
Sway Bar	Std.	——	——
Steering Recommended	Std.	——	——
Battery Recommended	Std.	——	——
Alternator	Std.	——	——
Turn Signal Flasher	Std.	——	——
Type Hitch Required	Body Mounted	——	——

1970 Trailer Towing Information

American Motors

Equipment	Class I	Class II	Class III
Trailer Type	Any	Any	Any
Tongue Load Limit (lbs)	250	350	500
Engine Requirement	232 cu in. Six	304 cu in. V-8	360 cu in. V-8
Exhaust System	Std.	Std.	Std.
Engine Cooling	H.D.	H.D.	H.D.
Transmission Requirement	Shift Command Automatic Transmission		
Trans. Aux. Oil Cooler Std V-8s Opt 6s	Required	Std.	Std.
Axle Ratio Recommended	Highest-Numerical Ratio for Particular Engine/Transmission combination		
Differential Type	Twin-Grip	Twin-Grip	Twin-Grip

1970 Trailer Towing Information (cont.)

American Motors

Equipment	Class I	Class II	Class III
Wheels Recommended	Std.	Std.	Std.
Tires		Largest size option for particular Model/Engine combination	
Brakes Recommended	Power	Power	Power
Front	Disc or drums	Disc or drums	Disc or drums
Rear	Drums	Drums	Drums
Springs	H.D.①	H.D.①	H.D.①
Shock Absorbers	H.D.①	H.D.①	H.D.①
Sway Bar	——	——	——
Steering Recommended	Power	Power	Power
Battery Recommended	H.D.②	H.D.②	H.D.②
Alternator	H.D.②	H.D.②	H.D.②
Turn Signal Flasher	H.D.②	H.D.②	H.D.②
Type Hitch Required	Body Mounted	Equalizer	Equalizer

① H.D.—Heavy duty; American Motor Handling Package.
② H.D.—Heavy duty; Electrical system.

1972 Trailer Towing Information

Jeep Truck 6000 and 7000 GVW Models

Equipment	Class I	Class II	Class III
Trailer Type	Any	Any	Any
Tongue Load Limit (lbs)	300	500	750
Engine Requirement	6000 GVW 304 cu in. V-8	360 cu in. V-8	360 cu in. V-8
	7000 GVW 360 cu in. V-8	360 cu in. V-8	360 cu in. V-8
Exhaust System	Std.	Std.	Std.
Engine Cooling	H.D.	H.D.	H.D.
Transmission Requirement	Automatic	Automatic	Automatic

1972 Trailer Towing Information (cont.)

Jeep Truck 6000 and 7000 GVW Models

Equipment	Class I	Class II	Class III
Trans. Aux. Oil Cooler	N.A.	N.A.	N.A.
Axle Ratio Recommended	Std.	Std.	Std.
Differential Type	Std.	Std.	Std.
Wheels Recommended	Std.	Std.	Std.
Tires	Std.	Std.	Std.
Brakes Recommended	Power	Power	Power
Front	Std.	Std.	Std.
Rear	Std.	Std.	Std.
Springs	H.D.	H.D.	H.D.
Shock Absorbers	H.D.	H.D.	H.D.
Sway Bar	N.A.	N.A.	N.A.
Steering Recommended	Power	Power	Power
Battery Recommended	Std.	Std.	H.D.
Alternator	Std.	Std.	H.D.
Turn Signal Flasher	Std.	Std.	H.D.
Type Hitch Required	Frame	Equalizer	Equalizer

Note: Prior to 1972 Jeep did not publish any trailer towing information.

1972 Trailer Towing Information

Jeep—8000 GVW Camper Special

Equipment	Class I	Class II	Class III
Trailer Type	Any	Any	Any
Tongue Load Limit (lbs)	300	500	750
Engine Requirement	304 cu in. V-8	360 cu in. V-8 Std.	360 cu in. V-8 Std.
Exhaust System	Std.	Std.	Std.
Engine Cooling	H.D. Std.	H.D. Std.	H.D. Std.

1972 Trailer Towing Information (cont.)

Jeep—8000 GVW Camper Special

Equipment	Class I	Class II	Class III
Transmission Requirement	Std.	Automatic	Automatic
Trans. Aux. Oil Cooler	N.A.	N.A.	N.A.
Axle Ratio Recommended	Std.	Std.	Std.
Differential Type	Std.	Std.	Std.
Wheels Recommended	Std.	Std.	Std.
Tires	7.50 x 16-E Range 10 Ply (Std.)		
Brakes Recommended	Power	Power	Power
Front	Std.	Std.	Std.
Rear	Std.	Std.	Std.
Springs	H.D. Std.	H.D. Std.	H.D. Std.
Shock Absorbers	H.D. Std.	H.D. Std.	H.D. Std.
Sway Bar	N.A.	N.A.	N.A.
Steering Recommended	Power	Power	Power
Battery Recommended	H.D.	H.D.	H.D.
Alternator	H.D.	H.D.	H.D.
Turn Signal Flasher	H.D.	H.D.	H.D.
Type Hitch Required	Frame	Equalizer	Equalizer

Note: Prior to 1972 Jeep did not publish any towing information.

1972 Trailer Towing Information

Jeep Wagoneer

Equipment	Class I	Class II	Class III
Trailer Type	Any	Any	Any
Tongue Load Limit (lbs)	300	500	750
Engine Requirement	304 cu in. V-8	360 cu in. V-8	360 cu in. V-8
Exhaust System	Std.	Std.	Std.

1972 Trailer Towing Information (cont.)

Jeep Wagoneer

Equipment	Class I	Class II	Class III
Engine Cooling	H.D.	H.D.	H.D.
Transmission Requirement	Automatic	Automatic	Automatic
Trans. Aux. Oil Cooler	N.A.	N.A.	N.A.
Axle Ratio Recommended	Highest-Numerical Ratio for particular Engine/Transmission Combination		
Differential Type	Std.	Std.	Std.
Wheels Recommended	Std.	Std.	Std.
Tires	Oversize	Oversize	Oversize
Brakes Recommended	Power	Power	Power
Front	Std.	Std.	Std.
Rear	Std.	Std.	Std.
Springs	H.D.	H.D.	H.D.
Shock Absorbers	H.D.	H.D.	H.D.
Sway Bar	——	——	——
Steering Recommended	Power	Power	Power
Battery Recommended	Std.	Std.	H.D.
Alternator	Std.	Std.	H.D.
Turn Signal Flasher	Std.	Std.	H.D.
Type Hitch Required	Equalizer	Equalizer	Equalizer

1972 Trailer Towing Information

Jeep (5000 GVW Models)

Equipment	Class I	Class II	Class III
Trailer Type	Any	Any	Any
Tongue Load Limit (lbs)	300	500	750
Engine Requirement	304 cu in. V-8	360 cu in. V-8	360 cu in. V-8

1972 Trailer Towing Information (cont.)

Jeep (5000 .GVW Models)

Equipment	Class I	Class II	Class III
Exhaust System	Std.	Std.	Std.
Engine Cooling	H.D.	H.D.	H.D.
Transmission Requirement	Automatic	Automatic	Automatic
Trans. Aux. Oil Cooler	N.A.	N.A.	N.A.
Axle Ratio Recommended	Highest-Numerical Ratio for particular Engine/Transmission Combination		
Differential Type	Std.	Std.	Std.
Wheels Recommended	Std.	Std.	Std.
Tires	Oversize	Oversize	Oversize
Brakes Recommended	Power	Power	Power
Front	Std.	Std.	Std.
Rear	Std.	Std.	Std.
Springs	H.D.	H.D.	H.D.
Shock Absorbers	H.D.	H.D.	H.D.
Sway Bar	——	——	——
Steering Recommended	Power	Power	Power
Battery Recommended	Std.	Std.	H.D.
Alternator	Std.	Std.	H.D.
Turn Signal Flasher	Std.	Std.	H.D.
Type Hitch Required	Equalizer	Equalizer	Equalizer

1972 Trailer Towing Information

Jeep CJ-5, CJ-6, Commando Standard GVW

Equipment	Class I	Class II	Class III
Trailer Type	Any	Any	Any
Tongue Load Limit (lbs)	300	500	750

1972 Trailer Towing Information (cont.)

Jeep CJ-5, CJ-6, Commando Standard GVW

Equipment	Class I	Class II	Class III
Engine Requirement	258 cu in. Six	304 cu in. V-8	304 cu in. V-8
Exhaust System	Std.	Std.	Std.
Engine Cooling	H.D.	H.D.	H.D.
Transmission Requirement	4-speed①	Std.①	Std.①
Trans. Aux. Oil Cooler	N.A.	N.A.	N.A.
Axle Ratio Recommended	Highest-Numerical Ratio for particular Engine/Transmission Combination		
Differential Type	Std.	Std.	Std.
Wheels Recommended	Std.	Std.	Std.
Tires	Oversize	Oversize	Oversize
Brakes Recommended	Power	Power	Power
Front	Std.	Std.	Std.
Rear	Std.	Std.	Std.
Springs	H.D.	H.D.	H.D.
Shock Absorbers	H.D.	H.D.	H.D.
Sway Bar	H.D.	H.D.	H.D.
Steering Recommended	Power	Power	Power
Battery Recommended	Std.	H.D.	H.D.
Alternator	Std.	H.D.	H.D.
Turn Signal Flasher	Std.	H.D.	H.D.
Type Hitch Required	Equalizer	Equalizer	Equalizer

① Automatic transmission in the Commando

1972 Trailer Towing Information
CJ-5, CJ-6, & Commando with Optional Heavy-Duty Package ▲

Equipment	Class I	Class II	Class III
Trailer Type	Any	Any	Any
Tongue Load Limit (lbs)	300	500	750
Engine Requirement	258 cu in. Six	304 cu in. V-8	304 cu in. V-8
Exhaust System	Std.	Std.	Std.
Engine Cooling	H.D.	H.D.	H.D.
Transmission Requirement	4 speed	Std.	Std.
Trans. Aux. Oil Cooler	N.A.	N.A.	N.A.
Axle Ratio Recommended	Highest-Numerical Ratio for particular Engine/Transmission Combination		
Differential Type	Std.	Std.	Std.
Wheels Recommended	H.D.	H.D.	H.D.
Tires	H.D.	H.D.	H.D.
Brakes Recommended	Power	Power	Power
Front	Std.	Std.	Std.
Rear	Std.	Std.	Std.
Springs	H.D.	H.D.	H.D.
Shock Absorbers	H.D.	H.D.	H.D.
Sway Bar	H.D.	H.D.	H.D.
Steering Recommended	Power	Power	Power
Battery Recommended	Std.	H.D.	H.D.
Alternator	Std.	H.D.	H.D.
Turn Signal Flasher	Std.	H.D.	H.D.
Type Hitch Required	Equalizer	Equalizer	Equalizer

▲ Optional GVW Package includes Extra Duty Front and Rear Suspension and 6.00 x 16-C Load Range 6-Ply All Service Tires on 16 in. Wheels with 4.5 in. E Rims.

1968–72 Trailer Towing Information

Cadillac ●

Equipment	Class I	Class II	Class III
Trailer Type	Any	Any	Any
Tongue Load Limit (lbs)	200	500	600
Engine Requirement	Std.	Std.	Std.
Exhaust System	Std.	Std.	Std.
Engine Cooling	Std.	H.D.	H.D.
Transmission Requirement	Std.	Std.	Std.
Trans. Aux. Oil Cooler	——	Required	Required
Axle Ratio Recommended	Std.	3.15:1	3.21:1
Differential Type	Std.	Std.	Std.
Wheels Recommended	Std.	Std.	H.D.
Tires	Std.	Std.	H.D.①
Brakes Recommended	Power Std.	Power Std.	Power Std.
Front	Std.	Std.	Std.
Rear	Std.	Std.	Std.
Springs	②	②	②
Shock Absorbers	②	②	②
Sway Bar	——	——	——
Steering Recommended	Std.	Std.	Std.
Battery Recommended	H.D.	H.D.	H.D.
Alternator	Std.	61 amp	61 amp
Turn Signal Flasher	H.D.	H.D.	H.D.
Type Hitch Required	Frame	Equalizer	Equalizer

●Eldorado is capable of towing a Class I trailer only.
① Load Range D
② Automatic Level Control for Class I, Automatic Level Control without A.L.C. Springs for Class II, A.L.C. with H.D. Springs for Class III

1972 Trailer Towing Information

Chevrolet ●

Equipment	Class I	Class II	Class III ▲
Trailer Type	Any	Any	Any
Tongue Load Limit (lbs)	200	350	500
Engine Requirement	350 cu in. V-8①	402 cu in. V-8	402 cu in. V-8⑤
Exhaust System	Std.	Std.	Std.
Engine Cooling	H.D.	H.D.	H.D.
Transmission Requirement	Turbo-Hydro②	Turbo-Hydro②	Turbo-Hydro
Trans. Aux. Oil Cooler	N.A.	N.A.	N.A.
Axle Ratio Recommended	3.08:1③	3.42:1④	3.42:1⑥
Differential Type	Positraction	Positraction	Positraction
Wheels Recommended	Std.	Std.	Std.
Tires	Std.	Std.	Std.
Brakes Recommended	Power	Power	Power
Front	Disc	Disc	Disc
Rear	Drum	Drum	Drum
Springs	H.D.	H.D.	H.D.
Shock Absorbers	H.D.	H.D.	H.D.
Sway Bar	——	——	——
Steering Recommended	Power	Power	Power
Battery Recommended	H.D.	H.D.	H.D.
Alternator	H.D.	H.D.	H.D.
Turn Signal Flasher	Std.	Std.	Std.
Type Hitch Required	Frame	Equalizer	Equalizer

● Except Camaro, Corvette and Vega
▲ Nova not recommended to tow Class III trailers
① 307 cu in. V-8 in Nova, Chevelle and El Camino.
② Standard Transmission in models other than full size.
③ 3.31:1 in models other than full size; 3.42:1 in Nova.
④ 2.73:1 in Chevelle and El Camino.
⑤ 454 cu in. in full size sedans.
⑥ 3.08:1 with 454 cu in. engine, 3.31:1 in Chevelle and El Camino.

1972 Trailer Towing Information

Camaro, Corvette, Vega

Equipment	Class I ▲	Class II ●	Class III ●
Trailer Type	Any	②	②
Tongue Load Limit (lbs)	100	②	②
Engine Requirement	Corvette 350 cu in. V-8	②	②
	Camaro 307 cu in. V-8	②	②
	Vega 140 cu in. 4 cyl	②	②
Exhaust System	Std	②	②
Engine Cooling	Std.	②	②
Transmission Requirement	Turbo-Hydro	②	②
Trans. Aux. Oil Cooler	——	②	②
Axle Ratio Recommended	Corvette 3.42:1	②	②
	Camaro 3.08:1	②	②
	Vega 3.36:1	②	②
Differential Type	Std.	②	②
Wheels Recommended	Std.	②	②
Tires	Std.	②	②
Brakes Recommended	Power	②	②
Front	Std.	②	②
Rear	Std.	②	②
Springs	Std.	②	②
Shock Absorbers	Std.	②	②
Sway Bar	Std.	②	②
Steering Recommended	Power	②	②
Battery Recommended	Std.	②	②
Alternator	Std.	②	②
Turn Signal Flasher	Std.	②	②
Type Hitch Required	Frame	②	②

▲ Up to 1,000 lbs.
● It is not recommended the Classes II and III type trailers be towed by these cars.
② Vehicle not recommended to tow Class II or Class III trailers.

1971 Trailer Towing Information

Chevrolet Trucks ▲

Equipment	Class I	Class II	Class III
Trailer Type	Any	Any	Any
Tongue Load Limit (lbs)	250	350	500
Engine Requirement		See Charts Next Page	
Exhaust System	Std.	Std.	Std.
Engine Cooling	Std.	Std.	Std.
Transmission Requirement	Turbo-Hydro	Turbo-Hydro	Turbo-Hydro
Trans. Aux. Oil Cooler	——	——	——
Axle Ratio Recommended		See Charts Next Page	
Differential Type	Std.	Std.	Std.
Wheels Recommended	Std.	Std.	Std.
Tires	①	①	①
Brakes Recommended	Power	Power	Power
Front	——	——	——
Rear	——	——	——
Springs	Std.	Std.	Std.
Shock Absorbers	Std.	Std.	Std.
Sway Bar	——	——	——
Steering Recommended	Std.	Std.	Std.
Battery Recommended	80 amp-hr	80 amp-hr	80 amp-hr
Alternator	42 amp	42 amp②	61 amp
Turn Signal Flasher	Std.	Std.	Std.
Type Hitch Required	Frame	Equalizer	Equalizer

▲ Suburban C-10, C-20, Pickup C-10, C-20, Blazer (AH), Sportvan G-10, G-20, G-30.
① Blazer, Pickup and Suburban C-10, H78 x 15B
Sportvan G-30, Pickup and Suburban C-20, 8.75 x 16.5C
Blazer K-10, G78 x 15B
Sportvan G-10, F78 x 14B
Sportvan G-20, 8.00 x 16.5C

1971 Trailer Towing Information (cont.)

Chevrolet Trucks

Suburban, Pickup Engine and Rear Axle Chart

Recommended Engine, Rear Axle Ratios and GCW for Trailer Towing
GCW—Combined Weight of Loaded Truck and Trailer—Lbs

Engine C10	4000	5000	6000	7000	GCW 8000	9000	10,000	11,000	12,000
250 cu in. Six	3.07	3.73	4.11						
292 cu in. Six		3.07	3.73	4.11					
307 cu in. V-8		3.07	3.73	4.11					
350 cu in. V-8				3.07		3.73	4.11		
400 cu in. V-8						3.07			
Engine C20									
250 cu in. Six		4.10	4.57						
292 cu in. Six			4.10	4.57					
307 cu in. V-8				4.10	4.57				
350 cu in. V-8						4.10	4.57		
400 cu in. V-8							3.54	4.10	

Blazer Engine and Rear Axle Chart

Recommended Engine, Rear Axle Ratios and GCW for Trailer Towing
GCW—Combined Weight of Loaded Truck and Trailer—Lbs

Engine C10	4000	5000	6000	7000	GCW 8000	9000	10,000	11,000	12,000
250 cu in. Six	3.07	3.73	4.11						
307 cu in. V-8		3.07	3.73	4.11					
350 cu in. V-8				3.07		3.73	4.11		
Engine K10									
250 cu in. Six		3.73							
307 cu in. V-8				3.73					
350 cu in. V-8				3.07		3.73			

Sportvan Engine and Rear Axle Chart

Recommended Engine, Rear Axle Ratios and GCW for Trailer Towing
GCW—Combined Weight of Loaded Truck and Trailer—Lbs

Engine G10	4000	5000	6000	7000	GCW 8000	9000	10,000	11,000	12,000
250 cu in. Six		3.36	3.73						
307 cu in. V-8		3.07	3.36	3.73					
Engine G20									
250 cu in. Six	3.36	3.73	4.11						
350 cu in. V-8				3.36		3.73			
Engine G30									
250 cu in. Six		4.10	4.57						
350 cu in. V-8						4.10	4.57		

1971 Trailer Towing Information

Chevrolet ▲

Equipment	Class I	Class II ●	Class III ■
Trailer Type	Any	Any	Any
Tongue Load Limit (lbs)	250	350	500
Engine Requirement	350 cu in. V-8①	402 cu in. V-8②	402 cu in. V-8
Exhaust System	Std.	Std.	Std.
Engine Cooling	H.D.	H.D.	H.D.
Transmission Requirement	Turbo-Hydro	Turbo-Hydro	Turbo-Hydro
Trans. Aux. Oil Cooler	——	——	——
Axle Ratio Recommended	3.08:1③	2.73:1④	3.42:1⑤
Differential Type	Positraction	Positraction	Positraction
Wheels Recommended	Std.	Std.	Std.
Tires	Std.	Std.	Std.
Brakes Recommended	Power	Power	Power
Front	Disc	Disc	Disc
Rear	Drum	Drum	Drum
Springs	H.D.	H.D.	H.D.
Shock Absorbers	H.D.	H.D.	H.D.
Sway Bar	——	——	——
Steering Recommended	Power	Power	Power
Battery Recommended	H.D.	H.D.	H.D.
Alternator	H.D.	H.D.	H.D.
Turn Signal Flasher	Std.	Std.	Std.
Type Hitch Required	Frame	Equalizer	Equalizer

▲ Except Vega, Camaro, Corvette.
● Monte Carlo is recommended only for Class I trailer towing.
■ Nova should not tow Class III trailers.
① 400 cu in. V-8 in full size sedans, 307 cu in. V-8 in Chevelle, El Camino and Nova.
② 350 cu in. V-8 in Nova.
③ 3.31:1 in Chevelle, El Camino and Monte Carlo, 3.36:1 in Nova.
④ 3.31:1 in Nova.
⑤ 3.31:1 in Chevelle and El Camino.

1971 Trailer Towing Information

Camaro, Corvette, Vega

Equipment	Class I ▲	Class II ●	Class III ●
Trailer Type	Any	——	——
Tongue Load Limit (lbs)	100	——	——
Engine Requirement	Camaro 307 cu in. V-8	——	——
	Corvette 350 cu in. V-8	——	——
	Vega 140 cu in. 4 cyl	——	——
Exhaust System	Std.	——	——
Engine Cooling	Std.	——	——
Transmission Requirement	Turbo-Hydro	——	——
Trans. Aux. Oil Cooler	——	——	——
Axle Ratio Recommended	3.08:1①	——	——
Differential Type	Std.	——	——
Wheels Recommended	Std.	——	——
Tires	Std.	——	——
Brakes Recommended	Power	——	——
Front	Std.	——	——
Rear	Std.	——	——
Springs	Std.	——	——
Shock Absorbers	Std.	——	——
Sway Bar	Std.	——	——
Steering Recommended	Power	——	——
Battery Recommended	Std.	——	——
Alternator	Std.	——	——
Turn Signal Flasher	Std.	——	——
Type Hitch Required	Frame	——	——

▲ Up to 1000 lbs.
● It is not recommended that Class II and III trailers be towed with Camaro, Corvette or Vega.
① 3.36:1 in Vega.

1971–'72 Trailer Towing Information

Charger, Coronet, Polara and Monaco

Equipment	Class I	Class II	Class III ▲
Trailer Type	Any	Any	Any
Tongue Load Limit (lbs)	250	350	500
Engine Requirement	318 cu in. V-8①	318 cu in. V-8①	318 cu in. V-8①
Exhaust System	Std.	Std.	Std.
Engine Cooling	H.D.	H.D.	H.D.
Transmission Requirement	TorqueFlite	TorqueFlite	TorqueFlite
Trans. Aux. Oil Cooler	——	——	——
Axle Ratio Recommended	3.23:1	3.23:1	3.23:1
Differential Type	Std.②	Std.②	Std.②
Wheels Recommended	H.D.	H.D.	H.D.
Tires	③	③	③
Brakes Recommended	Power	Power	Power
Front	Disc	Disc	Disc
Rear	Drum	Drum	Drum
Springs	H.D.	H.D.	H.D.
Shock Absorbers	H.D.	H.D.	H.D.
Sway Bar	Yes	Yes	Yes
Steering Recommended	Power	Power	Power
Battery Recommended	H.D. 70 amp	H.D. 70 amp	H.D. 70 amp
Alternator	H.D.	H.D.	H.D.
Turn Signal Flasher	H.D.	H.D.	H.D.
Type Hitch Required	Equalizer	Equalizer	Equalizer

▲ Up to 4,000 lbs gross.
① 383 cu in. 2 bbl and 4 bbl; 400 cu in. 2 bbl and 4 bbl in 1972 and 440 cu in. 4 bbl in 1971 are recommended options. 360 cu in. 2 bbl in Polara and Monaco.
② Sure Grip is a recommended option.
③ Charger G70 x 14; Coronet Wagons, H78 x 14; Polara and Monaco Wagons L84 x 15.

Chrysler—1968–1972

All Chryslers can be equipped with the following:

1. A larger radiator and a larger transmission oil cooler.
2. A seven-bladed fan and fan shroud and a radiator yoke-to-hood air seal (standard on air-conditioned models).
3. Heavy-duty suspension with larger front torsion bars and additional rear leaf springs.
4. An anti-sway bar and heavy-duty shock absorbers.
5. Heavy-duty stop lamp switch.
6. Heavy-duty turn signal flasher.
7. Heavy-duty drum brakes with 11 x 3 in. drums. Disc brakes are available on the New Yorker and the Town and Country Wagon.
8. Wider rims are also included.
9. Heavy-duty rear axle with a 3.23:1 ratio.

NOTE: *This package is mandatory for tow vehicles pulling trailers weighing 2500–5500 lbs.*

For 1973, Dodge offers three trailer towing packages which may be ordered separately or in combination with each other depending on the intended usage. The Wiring Package is available for pulling the camper type trailers or others of a reasonably light gross weight while the Heavy-Duty package may also be ordered.

The Trailer Towing Package basically consists of all the items in the Heavy-Duty and the Wiring Packages, plus an externally-mounted transmission oil cooler and a 3.23:1 ratio rear axle.

The Heavy-Duty package consists of a Cooling Package (larger radiator, fan shroud, and coolant reserve system); Heavy-Duty Suspension (larger front sway bar, larger torsion bars, higher rear leaf spring rate), and extra wide wheel rims.

The Wiring Package includes a 60 ampere heavy-duty alternator and a heavy-duty stop lamp switch, a variable-load turn signal flasher, and a trailer wiring harness. This is a seven-wire harness with wires for ground, right stop and turn signal; left stop and turn signal; taillights, license and side marker lights, back-up lamp, electric trailer brake, and auxiliary.

Dodge offers a variety of class I and II hitches for towing light and medium trailers and they are available for all Dodge vehicles. It should be noted that all the hitches are dealer-installed items.

Trailer Towing Information

1972 Ford (Mustang, Maverick, Pinto)

Equipment	Class I	Class II	Class III
Trailer Type	*	—	—
Tongue Load Limit (lbs)	200 lbs.	—	—
Engine Requirement	**	—	—
Exhaust System	Std.	—	—
Engine Cooling	Std.	—	—
Transmission Requirement	Cruise-o-matic	—	—
Trans. Aux. Oil Cooler	—	—	—

Trailer Towing Information

1972 Ford (Mustang, Maverick, Pinto)

Equipment	Class I	Class II	Class III
Axle Ratio Recommended	Std. for Mustang & Pinto Mustang: 3.25:1 Maverick: 3.00:1 ——		——
Differential Type	Std.	——	——
Wheels Recommended	Std.	——	——
Tires	Std.	——	——
Brakes Recommended	Power front for Mustang Std. for others ——		——
Front	Std.	——	——
Rear	Std.	——	——
Springs	Std.	——	——
Shock Absorbers	Std.	——	——
Sway Bar	Std.	——	——
Steering Recommended	Power Steering Recommended for Mustang ——		——
Battery Recommended	Std.	——	——
Alternator	Std.	——	——
Turn Signal Flasher	Std.	——	——
Type Hitch Required	Non-Equalizing ①	——	——

* Trailers with frontal area less than 25 sq. ft.
** Maverick uses a 200 cu in. 6 cyl.
Pinto uses a 2000 cc. engine
Mustang uses a 302 cu in. V-8 for Trailers with less than 250 sq ft of frontal area and a 351 cu in. V-8 for over 25 sq ft in frontal area.
① Never use a bumper mounted hitch on these units.

1972 Trailer Towing Information

Torino, Ranchero

Equipment	Class I	Class II	Class III
Trailer Type	Any	Any	Any
Tongue Load Limit (lbs)	200	500	700
Engine Requirement	302 cu in. V-8①	351 cu in. V-8①	400 cu in. V-8①
Exhaust System	Std.	Std.	Std.
Engine Cooling	H.D.	H.D.	H.D.
Transmission Requirement	Cruise-O-Matic	Cruise-O-Matic	Cruise-O-Matic
Trans. Aux. Oil Cooler	——	——	——
Axle Ratio Recommended	Std.	Std.	3.25:1
Differential Type	Std.	Std.	Std.
Wheels Recommended	Std.	Std.	Std.
Tires	Std.	F78 x 14	G78 x 14
Brakes Recommended	Std.	Power	Power
Front	Std.	Disc	Disc
Rear	Std.	Drum	Drum
Springs	Std.	H.D.	H.D.
Shock Absorbers	Std.	H.D.	H.D.
Sway Bar	——	——	——
Steering Recommended	Std.	Power	Power
Battery Recommended	Std.	Std.	H.D.
Alternator	Std.	Std.	H.D.
Turn Signal Flasher	Std.	Std.	Std.
Type Hitch Required	Frame	Equalizer	Equalizer

① Mountainous driving, it is recommended that the larger engines be used (400 cu in. V-8 and 429 cu in. V-8).

1972 Trailer Towing Information

Ford

Equipment	Class I	Class II	Class III
Trailer Type	Any	Any	Any
Tongue Load Limit (lbs)	200	500	900
Engine Requirement	351 cu in. V-8	351 cu in. V-8	351 cu in. V-8
Exhaust System	Std.	Std.	Std.
Engine Cooling	Std.	H.D.	H.D.
Transmission Requirement	Std.	Std.	Std.
Trans. Aux. Oil Cooler	——	——	——
Axle Ratio Recommended	Std.	Std.	Std.
Differential Type	Std.	Std.	Std.
Wheels Recommended	Std.	Std.	H.D.
Tires	Std.	Std.	Std.
Brakes Recommended	Power	Power	Power
Front	Std.	Std.	Std.
Rear	Std.	Std.	Std.
Springs	Std.	H.D.	H.D.①
Shock Absorbers	Std.	H.D.	H.D.
Sway Bar	——	——	——
Steering Recommended	Std.	Power	Power
Battery Recommended	Std.	Std.	H.D.
Alternator	Std.	Std.	H.D.
Turn Signal Flasher	Std.	Std.	Std.
Type Hitch Required	Frame	Equalizer	Equalizer

① Heavy-duty frame.

Trailer Towing Information

1972 (Mercury Monterey, Marquis)

Equipment	Class I	Class II	Class III
Trailer Type	Any	Any	Any
Tongue Load Limit (lbs)	to 200 lbs	200 to 500 lbs	350 to 900 lbs
Engine Requirement	Std.	400 V-8	400 V-8
Exhaust System	Std.	Std.	Std.
Engine Cooling	Extra cooling package	Std.	Std.
Transmission Requirement	Std.	Std.	Std.
Trans. Aux. Oil Cooler	——	——	——
Axle Ratio Recommended	Std.	Std.	Std.
Differential Type	Std.	Std.	Std.
Wheels Recommended	Std.	Std.	Std.
Tires	Std.	Std.	Std.
Brakes Recommended	Std.	Std.	Std.
Front	Std.	Std.	Std.
Rear	Std.	Std.	Std.
Springs	Std.	Std.	Std.
Shock Absorbers	Std.	Std.	Std.
Sway Bar	Std.	Std.	Std.
Steering Recommended	Std.	Std.	Std.
Battery Recommended	Std.	Std.	Std.
Alternator	Std.	Std.	Std.
Turn Signal Flasher	Std.	Std.	Std.
Type Hitch Required	Frame①	Equalizer	Equalizer

Trailer Towing Information

1972 Mercury Cougar

Equipment	Class I	Class II	Class III
Trailer Type	Any	——	——
Tongue Load Limit (lbs)	to 200 lbs	——	——
Engine Requirement	Recommend 351-2V	——	——
Exhaust System	Std.	——	——
Engine Cooling	Std.	——	——
Transmission Requirement	Select-Shift is recommended	——	——
Trans. Aux. Oil Cooler	Recommended	——	——
Axle Ratio Recommended	3.00:1	——	——
Differential Type	Std.	——	——
Wheels Recommended	Std.	——	——
Tires	Std.	——	——
Brakes Recommended	Std.	——	——
Front	Std.	——	——
Rear	Std.	——	——
Springs	Std.	——	——
Shock Absorbers	Air shocks are available	——	——
Sway Bar	——	——	——
Steering Recommended	Power	——	——
Battery Recommended	Std.	——	——
Alternator	Std.	——	——
Turn Signal Flasher	Std.	——	——
Type Hitch Required	Non-equalizing	——	——

Trailer Towing Information

1972 Mercury Comet

Equipment	Class I	Class II	Class III
Trailer Type	Any	——	——
Tongue Load Limit (lbs)	to 200 lbs	——	——
Engine Requirement	*	——	——
Exhaust System	Std.	——	——
Engine Cooling	Std.	——	——
Transmission Requirement	Select-Shift Automatic	——	——
Trans. Aux. Oil Cooler	——	——	——
Axle Ratio Recommended	3.00:1	——	——
Differential Type	Std.	——	——
Wheels Recommended	Std.	——	——
Tires	Std.	——	——
Brakes Recommended	Std.	——	——
Front	Std.	——	——
Rear	Std.	——	——
Springs	**	——	——
Shock Absorbers	**	——	——
Sway Bar	**	——	——
Steering Recommended	Power	——	——
Battery Recommended	55 amp	——	——
Alternator	Std.	——	——
Turn Signal Flasher	Std.	——	——
Type Hitch Required	Non-equalizing	——	——

* 200 cu in. engine is sufficient for trailer with frontal area less than 25 sq. ft.;
302 cu in. engine is sufficient for trailer with frontal area more than 25 sq. ft.
** A handling package is available.

Trailer Towing Information

1972 Thunderbird

Equipment	Class I	Class II	Class III
Trailer Type	Any	Any	Any
Tongue Load Limit (lbs)	up to 200 lbs	200 to 350 lbs	350 to 700 lbs
Engine Requirement	429 4V V-8	429 4V V-8	429 4V V-8
Exhaust System	Std.	Std.	Std.
Engine Cooling	Special cooling system is available		
Transmission Requirement	Std.	Std.	Std.
Trans. Aux. Oil Cooler	——	——	——
Axle Ratio Recommended	3.25:1	3.25:1	3.25:1
Differential Type	Std.	Std.	Std.
Wheels Recommended	Std.	Std.	Std.
Tires	Std.	Std.	Std.
Brakes Recommended	Std.	Std.	Std.
Front	Std.	Std.	Std.
Rear	Std.	Std.	Std.
Springs	*	*	*
Shock Absorbers	*	*	*
Sway Bar	——	——	——
Steering Recommended	Std.	Std.	Std.
Battery Recommended	Std.	Std.	Std.
Alternator	Std.	Std.	Std.
Turn Signal Flasher	*	*	*
Type Hitch Required	Frame	Equalizing	Equalizing

* Trailer Towing Package Includes:
(1) Extra Cooling Components
(2) Wiring Harness
(3) Heavy Duty Suspension
(4) 3.25:1 Rear Axle Ratio

Trailer Towing Information

1972 Mercury Montego

Equipment	Class I	Class II	Class III
Trailer Type	Any	Any	Any
Tongue Load Limit (lbs)	to 200 lbs	200 to 500 lbs	500 to 900 lbs
Engine Requirement	Std.	351 cu in.	400 cu in.
Exhaust System	Std.	Std.	Std.
Engine Cooling	Std.	Std.	Std.
Transmission Requirement		Select-Shift Automatic	
Trans. Aux. Oil Cooler	——	——	——
Axle Ratio Recommended	Std.	3.25:1	3.25:1
Differential Type	Std.	Std.	Std.
Wheels Recommended	Std.	Std.	Std.
Tires	Std.	Std.	G78-14
Brakes Recommended	Std.	Power Disc	Power Disc
Front	Std.	Std.	Std.
Rear	Std.	Std.	Std.
Springs	*	**	***
Shock Absorbers	*	**	***
Sway Bar	*	**	***
Steering Recommended	Std.	Power	Power
Battery Recommended	Std.	Std.	Std.
Alternator	Std.	Std.	Std.
Turn Signal Flasher	Std.	Std.	Std.
Type Hitch Required	Frame	Equalizer	Equalizer

* Cross country ride package is recommended for Class I trailers.
** Medium Duty Towing Package.
*** Optional Trailer Towing Package.

1971 Trailer Towing Information

Thunderbird

Equipment	Class I	Class II	Class III
Trailer Type	Any	Any	Any
Tongue Load Limit (lbs)	200	350	700
Engine Requirement	429 cu in. V-8	429 cu in. V-8	429 cu in. V-8①
Exhaust System	Std.	Std.	Std.
Engine Cooling	Std.	H.D.	H.D.
Transmission Requirement	Std.	Std.	Std.
Trans. Aux. Oil Cooler	——	——	——
Axle Ratio Recommended	2.75:1	3.25:1	3.25:1
Differential Type	Traction-Lok	Traction-Lok	Traction-Lok
Wheels Recommended	Std.	Std.	Std.
Tires	Std.	Std.	Std.
Brakes Recommended	Power	Power	Power
Front	Disc	Disc	Disc
Rear	Drum	Drum	Drum
Springs	Std.②	H.D.③	H.D.③
Shock Absorbers	Std.	H.D.	H.D.
Sway Bar	——	——	——
Steering Recommended	Std.	Std.	Std.
Battery Recommended	H.D.	H.D.	H.D.
Alternator	H.D.	H.D.	H.D.
Turn Signal Flasher	Std.	Std.	Std.
Type Hitch Required	Frame	Equalizer	Equalizer

① 4 bbl carburetor recommended.
② With Automatic ride control.
③ Without Automatic ride control.

1971 Trailer Towing Information

Maverick

Equipment	Class I	Class II	Class III
Trailer Type	Any	①	①
Tongue Load Limit (lbs)	200	①	①
Engine Requirement	200 cu in. Six	①	①
Exhaust System	Std.	①	①
Engine Cooling	Std.	①	①
Transmission Requirement	Cruise-O-Matic	①	①
Trans. Aux. Oil Cooler	——	①	①
Axle Ratio Recommended	3.00:1	①	①
Differential Type	Std.	①	①
Wheels Recommended	Std.	①	①
Tires	Std.	①	①
Brakes Recommended	Std.	①	①
Front	Std.	①	①
Rear	Std.	①	①
Springs	Std.	①	①
Shock Absorbers	Std.	①	①
Sway Bar	——	①	①
Steering Recommended	Std.	①	①
Battery Recommended	Std.	①	①
Alternator	Std.	①	①
Turn Signal Flasher	Std.	①	①
Type Hitch Required	Frame	①	①

① It is not recommended that the Maverick tow Class II or III trailers.

1971 Trailer Towing Information

Mustang, Comet

Equipment	Class I	Class II	Class III
Trailer Type	Any	④	④
Tongue Load Limit (lbs)	200	④	④
Engine Requirement	351 cu in. V-8①	④	④
Exhaust System	Std.	④	④
Engine Cooling	Std.	④	④
Transmission Requirement	Cruise-O-Matic	④	④
Trans. Aux. Oil Cooler	——	④	④
Axle Ratio Recommended	3.00:1	④	④
Differential Type	Std.	④	④
Wheels Recommended	Std.	④	④
Tires	Std.	④	④
Brakes Recommended	Std.	④	④
Front	Std.	④	④
Rear	Std.	④	④
Springs	Std.②	④	④
Shock Absorbers	Std.②	④	④
Sway Bar	——	④	④
Steering Recommended	Std.	④	④
Battery Recommended	Std.③	④	④
Alternator	Std.	④	④
Turn Signal Flasher	Std.	④	④
Type Hitch Required	Frame	④	④

① 250 cu in. Six in Comet.
② H.D. in Comet.
③ 55 Amp in Comet.
④ Not recommended for Class II or Class III trailers.

1971 Trailer Towing Information

Ford

Equipment	Class I	Class II	Class III
Trailer Type	Any	Any	Any
Tongue Load Limit (lbs)	200	500	700
Engine Requirement	240 cu in. Six	400 cu in. V-8	400 cu in. V-8
Exhaust System	Std.	Std.	Std.
Engine Cooling	Std.	H.D.	H.D.
Transmission Requirement	Cruise-O-Matic	Cruise-O-Matic	Cruise-O-Matic
Trans. Aux. Oil Cooler	——	——	——
Axle Ratio Recommended	2.75:1	3.25:1	3.25:1
Differential Type	Traction-Lok	Traction-Lok	Traction-Lok
Wheels Recommended	Std.	6.5 x 15	6.5 x 15
Tires	Std.	H78 x 15①	H78 x 15①
Brakes Recommended	Std.	Power	Power
Front	Std.	Disc	Disc
Rear	Std.	Drum	Drum
Springs	Std.	H.D.	H.D.
Shock Absorbers	Std.	H.D.	H.D.
Sway Bar	——	——	——
Steering Recommended	Std.	Power	Power
Battery Recommended	Std.	80 amp	80 amp
Alternator	Std.	55 amp	55 amp
Turn Signal Flasher	Std.	Std.	Std.
Type Hitch Required	Frame	Equalizer	Equalizer

① Standard size on wagons.

1971 Trailer Towing Information

Torino

Equipment	Class I	Class II	Class III
Trailer Type	Any	Any	①
Tongue Load Limit (lbs)	200	350	①
Engine Requirement	351 cu in. V-8	351 cu in. V-8	①
Exhaust System	Std.	Std.	①
Engine Cooling	Std.	H.D.	①
Transmission Requirement	Cruise-O-Matic	Cruise-O-Matic	①
Trans. Aux. Oil Cooler	——	——	①
Axle Ratio Recommended	3.00:1	3.25:1	①
Differential Type	Traction-Lok	Traction-Lok	①
Wheels Recommended	Std.	Std.	①
Tires	Std.	F78 x 14	①
Brakes Recommended	Power	Power	①
Front	Disc	Disc	①
Rear	Drum	Drum	①
Springs	Std.	H.D.	①
Shock Absorbers	Std.	H.D.	①
Sway Bar	——	——	①
Steering Recommended	Std.	Power	①
Battery Recommended	Std.	70 amp	①
Alternator	Std.	55 amp	①
Turn Signal Flasher	Std.	Std.	①
Type Hitch Required	Frame	Equalizer	①

① Vehicle is not recommended to tow Class III trailers.

1971 Trailer Towing Information

Montego, Cyclone

Equipment	Class I	Class II	Class III ●
Trailer Type	Any	Any	——
Tongue Load Limit (lbs)	200	350	——
Engine Requirement	302 cu in. V-8	351 cu in. V-8	——
Exhaust System	Std.	Std.	——
Engine Cooling	Std.	H.D.	——
Transmission Requirement	Select-Shift	Select-Shift	——
Trans. Aux. Oil Cooler	——	——	——
Axle Ratio Recommended	3.00:1	3.25:1	——
Differential Type	Std.	Std.	——
Wheels Recommended	Std.	Std.	——
Tires	Std.	Std.	——
Brakes Recommended	Power	Power	——
Front	Disc	Disc	——
Rear	Drum	Drum	——
Springs	Std.①	H.D.	——
Shock Absorbers	Std.	H.D.	——
Sway Bar	——	——	——
Steering Recommended	Power	Power	——
Battery Recommended	Std.	70 amp	——
Alternator	Std.	55 amp	——
Turn Signal Flasher	Std.	Std.	——
Type Hitch Required	Frame	Equalizer	——

● It is not recommended that these cars tow a Class III trailer.
① Air springs recommended without Equalizer hitch.

1971 Trailer Towing Information

Marquis, Marauder, Monterey

Equipment	Class I	Class II	Class III
Trailer Type	Any	Any	Any
Tongue Load Limit (lbs)	200	500	700
Engine Requirement	400 cu in. V-8	400 cu in. V-8	400 cu in. V-8
Exhaust System	Std.	Std.	Std.
Engine Cooling	H.D.	H.D.	H.D.
Transmission Requirement	Select-Shift	Select-Shift	Select-Shift
Trans. Aux. Oil Cooler	——	——	——
Axle Ratio Recommended	3.25:1	3.25:1	3.25:1
Differential Type	Std.	Std.	Std.
Wheels Recommended	Std.	Std.	Std.
Tires	H78 x 15	H78 x 15	H78 x 15
Brakes Recommended	Power	Power	Power
Front	Disc	Disc	Disc
Rear	Drum	Drum	Drum
Springs	Std.	H.D.	H.D.
Shock Absorbers	Std.	H.D.	H.D.
Sway Bar	——	——	——
Steering Recommended	Power	Power	Power
Battery Recommended	Std.	80 amp/hr	80 amp/hr
Alternator	Std.	55 amp	Std.
Turn Signal Flasher	Std.	Std.	Std.
Type Hitch Required	Frame	Equalizer	Equalizer

1971 Trailer Towing Information

Cougar

Equipment	Class I	Class II ●	Class III ●
Trailer Type	Any	——	——
Tongue Load Limit (lbs)	200	——	——
Engine Requirement	351 cu in. V-8	——	——
Exhaust System	Std.	——	——
Engine Cooling	H.D.	——	——
Transmission Requirement	Select-Shift	——	——
Trans. Aux. Oil Cooler	Yes	——	——
Axle Ratio Recommended	3.00:1	——	——
Differential Type	Std.	——	——
Wheels Recommended	Std.	——	——
Tires	Std.	——	——
Brakes Recommended	Power	——	——
Front	Disc	——	——
Rear	Drum	——	——
Springs	Std.①	——	——
Shock Absorbers	Std.	——	——
Sway Bar	——	——	——
Steering Recommended	Power	——	——
Battery Recommended	Std.	——	——
Alternator	Std.	——	——
Turn Signal Flasher	Std.	——	——
Type Hitch Required	Frame	——	——

● It is not recommended that this car tow a Class II or III trailer.
① Air springs recommended if without Equalizer hitch.

1971 Trailer Towing Information

Continental, Mark III

Equipment	Class I	Class II	Class III
Trailer Type	Any	Any	Any
Tongue Load Limit (lbs)	200	500	700
Engine Requirement	460 cu in. V-8	460 cu in. V-8	460 cu in. V-8
Exhaust System	Std.	Std.	Std.
Engine Cooling	Std.	Std.	Std.
Transmission Requirement	Select-Shift	Select-Shift	Select-Shift
Trans. Aux. Oil Cooler	——	——	——
Axle Ratio Recommended	2.80:1	3.00:1	3.00:1
Differential Type	Std.	Std.	Std.
Wheels Recommended	Std.	Std.	Std.
Tires	Std.	Std.	Std.
Brakes Recommended	Power	Power	Power
Front	Disc	Disc	Disc
Rear	Drum	Drum	Drum
Springs	Std.	Std.	H.D.
Shock Absorbers	Std.	Std.	H.D.
Sway Bar	——	——	——
Steering Recommended	Power	Power	Power
Battery Recommended	Std.	Std.	Std.
Alternator	Std.	Std.	Std.
Turn Signal Flasher	Std.	Std.	Std.
Type Hitch Required	Frame	Equalizer	Equalizer

1970 Trailer Towing Information

Marquis, Marauder, Monterey

Equipment	Class I	Class II	Class III
Trailer Type	Any	Any	Any
Tongue Load Limit (lbs)	200	500	700
Engine Requirement	390 cu in. V-8	429 cu in. V-8	429 cu in. V-8
Exhaust System	Std.	Std.	Std.
Engine Cooling	Std.	H.D.	H.D.
Transmission Requirement	Select-Shift	Select-Shift	Select-Shift
Trans. Aux. Oil Cooler	——	——	——
Axle Ratio Recommended	2.75:1	3.25:1	3.25:1
Differential Type	Std.	Std.	Std.
Wheels Recommended	Std.	Std.	Std.
Tires	H78 x 15	H78 x 15	H78 x 15
Brakes Recommended	Power	Power	Power
Front	Disc	Disc	Disc
Rear	Drum	Drum	Drum
Springs	Std.	H.D.	H.D.
Shock Absorbers	Std.	H.D.	H.D.
Sway Bar	——	——	——
Steering Recommended	Power	Power	Power
Battery Recommended	Std.	H.D. 80 amp	H.D. 80 amp
Alternator	Std.	65 amp	65 amp
Turn Signal Flasher	Std.	Std.	Std.
Type Hitch Required	Frame	Equalizer	Equalizer

1970 Trailer Towing Information

Montego, Cyclone

Equipment	Class I	Class II	Class III
Trailer Type	Any	Any	②
Tongue Load Limit (lbs)	200	350	②
Engine Requirement	302 cu in. V-8	351 cu in. V-8	②
Exhaust System	Std.	Std.	②
Engine Cooling	Std.	H.D.	②
Transmission Requirement	Select-Shift	Select-Shift	②
Trans. Aux. Oil Cooler	——	——	②
Axle Ratio Recommended	3.00:1	3.25:1	②
Differential Type	Std.	Std.	②
Wheels Recommended	Std.	Std.	②
Tires	Std.	Std.	②
Brakes Recommended	Power	Power	②
Front	Disc	Disc	②
Rear	Drum	Drum	②
Springs	Std.①	H.D.	②
Shock Absorbers	Std.	H.D.	②
Sway Bar	——	——	②
Steering Recommended	Power	Power	②
Battery Recommended	Std.	70 amp	②
Alternator	Std.	55 amp	②
Turn Signal Flasher	Std.	Std.	②
Type Hitch Required	Frame	Equalizer	②

① Air springs recommended.
② It is not recommended that these cars tow Class III trailers.

Trailer Towing Information

1972 Oldsmobile (F-85, Cutlass, Cutlass S,
Cutlass Supreme and Vista Cruiser)

Equipment	Class I	Class II	Class III
Trailer Type	Any	Any	Vista Cruiser only
Tongue Load Limit (lbs)	to 200 lbs	to 350 lbs	to 600 lbs
Engine Requirement	350 V-8	350 V-8	455 V-8
Exhaust System	Std.	Std.	Std.
Engine Cooling	H.D. System (Recommended)	H.D. System (Required)	H.D. System (Required)
Transmission Requirement	Turbo-Hydra-Matic 350	Turbo-Hydra-Matic 350	Turbo-Hydra-Matic 400
Trans. Aux. Oil Cooler	Available	Available	Recommended
Axle Ratio Recommended	3.08:1	3.08:1	3.23:1
Differential Type	Std.	Std.	Std.
Wheels Recommended	H.D. Required	H.D. Required	H.D. Required
Tires	Std.	Std.	Std.
Brakes Recommended	Std.	Std.	Std.
Front	Std.	Std.	Std.
Rear	Std.	Std.	Std.
Springs	*	*	*
Shock Absorbers	*	*	*
Sway Bar	*	*	*
Steering Recommended	Std.	Std.	Std.
Battery Recommended	Std.	Std.	Std.
Alternator	Std.	Std.	Std.
Turn Signal Flasher	**	**	**
Type Hitch Required	Frame	Equalizer	Equalizer

* H.D. Suspension is available. It is recommended for all Class II trailers and required for Class III.
** Trailer wiring harness is recommended.

Trailer Towing Information

1972 Oldsmobile (Delta 88, Custom Cruiser,
Ninety-Eight, Toronado Custom)

Equipment	Class I	Class II	Class III
Trailer Type	Any	Any	Any
Tongue Load Limit (lbs)	to 200 lbs	to 350 lbs	to 600 lbs
Engine Requirement	Std.	455 V-8	455 V-8
Exhaust System	Std.	Dual	Dual
Engine Cooling	H.D. System Recommended	H.D. System Required	H.D. System Required
Transmission Requirement	Turbo-Hydra-Matic 400		
Trans. Aux. Oil Cooler	Available	Available	Recommended
Axle Ratio Recommended	Std.	2.93:1	3.23:1 for all except Toronado which uses a 3.07:1 Ratio
Differential Type	Std.	Std.	Std.
Wheels Recommended	Std.*	Std.*	Std.
Tires	Std.	Std.	Std.
Brakes Recommended	Std.	Std.	Std.
Front	Std.	Std.	Std.
Rear	Std.	Std.	Std.
Springs	**	**	**
Shock Absorbers	**	**	**
Sway Bar	**	**	**
Steering Recommended	Std.	Std.	Std.
Battery Recommended	Std.	Std.	Std.
Alternator	Std.	Std.	Std.
Turn Signal Flasher	***	***	***
Type Hitch Required	Frame	Equalizing	Equalizing

* Delta 88 and Ninety-Eight require the use of H.D. wheels.
** A suspension package is recommended.
*** Trailer wiring harness recommended.

Trailer Towing Information

1972 Oldsmobile (F-85, Cutlass, Cutlass S, Cutlass Supreme, 4-4-2, Vista Cruiser)

Equipment	Class I	Class II	Class III
Trailer Type	Any	Any	Only Vista Cruiser
Tongue Load Limit (lbs)	to 200 lbs	200 to 350 lbs	350 to 600 lbs
Engine Requirement	350 V-8	350 V-8	455 V-8
Exhaust System	Std.	Std.	Std.
Engine Cooling	H.D. System Recommended	H.D. System Required	H.D. System Required
Transmission Requirement	Turbo-Hydra-Matic 350 Recommended	Turbo-Hydra-Matic 350 Required	Turbo-Hydra-Matic 400 Required
Trans. Aux. Oil Cooler	——	——	——
Axle Ratio Recommended	3.08:1 Recommended	3.08:1 Required	3.08:1 Required
Differential Type	Anti-Spin Axle Available		
Wheels Recommended	Std.	Std.	Std.
Tires	Std.	Std.	Std.
Brakes Recommended	Std.	Std.	Std.
Front	Std.	Std.	Std.
Rear	Std.	Std.	Std.
Springs	H.D. System Available	H.D. System Required	H.D. System Required
Shock Absorbers	H.D. units Available		
Sway Bar	——	——	——
Steering Recommended	Std.	Std.	Std.
Battery Recommended	Std.	Std.	Std.
Alternator	Std.	Std.	Std.
Turn Signal Flasher	Std.	Std.	Std.
Type Hitch Required	Frame	Equalizing	Equalizing

Trailer Towing Information

1971 Oldsmobile (Delta 88 [Custom Royale], Custom Cruiser, Ninety Eight and Luxury Toronado)

Equipment	Class I	Class II	Class III
Trailer Type	Any	Any	Any
Tongue Load Limit (lbs)	to 200 lbs	200 to 350 lbs	350 to 600 lbs
Engine Requirement	Std.	455 V-8 Required	455 V-8 Required
Exhaust System	Std.	Dual	Dual
Engine Cooling	H.D. System Recommended	H.D. System Required	H.D. System Required
Transmission Requirement	Turbo-Hydra-Matic 350 Recommended	Turbo-Hydra-Matic 400 Required	Turbo-Hydra-Matic 400 Required
Trans. Aux. Oil Cooler	——	——	——
Axle Ratio Recommended	Std.	3.08:1 or 3.42:1 Required	3.42:1 Required
Differential Type	Std.	Std.	Std.
Wheels Recommended	H.D.	H.D. Recommended	H.D. Required
Tires	Std.	Std.	Std.
Brakes Recommended	Std.	Std.	Std.
Front	Std.	Std.	Std.
Rear	Std.	Std.	Std.
Springs	❊	❊	❊
Shock Absorbers	H.D. units are Available		
Sway Bar	❊	❊	❊
Steering Recommended	Std.	Std.	Std.
Battery Recommended	Std.	Std.	Std.
Alternator	Std.	Std.	Std.
Turn Signal Flasher	Std.	Std.	Std.
Type Hitch Required	Frame	Equalizer	Equalizer

❊ Heavy Duty Suspension is available.
Note: The trailer wiring harness is recommended.

Trailer Towing Information

1970 Oldsmobile (Vista Cruiser, 4-4-2, Cutlass Supreme, Cutlass S, Cutlass and F-85)

Equipment	Class I	Class II	Class III
Trailer Type	Any	Any	Vista Cruiser
Tongue Load Limit (lbs)	to 200 lbs	200 to 350 lbs	350 to 600 lbs
Engine Requirement	350 V-8	350 V-8	455 V-8
Exhaust System	Std.	Std.	Std.
Engine Cooling	H.D. System Recommended	H.D. System Required	H.D. System Required
Transmission Requirement	Turbo-Hydra-Matic 350 Recommended	Turbo-Hydra-Matic 350 Required	Turbo-Hydra-Matic 400 Required
Trans. Aux. Oil Cooler	Recommended	Required	Required
Axle Ratio Recommended	3.08:1 Recommended	3.08:1 Required	3.08:1 Required
Differential Type	Anti-Spin Available		
Wheels Recommended	Std.	Std.	Std.
Tires	Std.	Std.	Std.
Brakes Recommended	Power Front Disc (Recommended)		
Front	Disc	Disc	Disc
Rear	Drum	Drum	Drum
Springs	*	*	*
Shock Absorbers	H.D. units are Available		
Sway Bar	*	*	*
Steering Recommended	Vari-Ratio Steering Available		
Battery Recommended	Std.	Std.	Std.
Alternator	Std.	Std.	Std.
Turn Signal Flasher	**	**	**
Type Hitch Required	Frame	Equalizer	Equalizer

* H.D. Suspension is recommended for all units.
** Trailer wiring harness is recommended.

Trailer Towing Information

1970 Oldsmobile (Toronado, Ninety-Eight, Delta Series Cars)

Equipment	Class I	Class II	Class III
Trailer Type	Any	Any	Any
Tongue Load Limit (lbs)	to 200 lbs	200 to 350 lbs	350 to 600 lbs
Engine Requirement	350 V-8	455 V-8	455 V-8
Exhaust System	Std.	Std.	Std.
Engine Cooling	H.D. System Required		
Transmission Requirement	Std.	Std.	Std.
Trans. Aux. Oil Cooler	Recommended	Required	Required
Axle Ratio Recommended	Std.	2.93:1 Required on All 98 Series	2.93:1 Required in all Delta Series
Differential Type	Std.	Anti-Spin Available	Anti-Spin Available
Wheels Recommended	Std.	Std.	Std.
Tires	Std.	Std.	Std.
Brakes Recommended	Front Disc Std.	Front Disc Std.	Front Disc Std.
Front	Disc	Disc	Disc
Rear	Drum	Drum	Drum
Springs	*	*	*
Shock Absorbers	H.D. units available		
Sway Bar	*	*	*
Steering Recommended	Std.	Std.	Std.
Battery Recommended	Std.	Std.	Std.
Alternator	Std.	Std.	Std.
Turn Signal Flasher	**	**	**
Type Hitch Required	Frame	Equalizing	Equalizing

* H.D. Suspension is available for all models.
** Trailer wiring harness is available.

Trailer Towing Information

1969 Oldsmobile (Toronado, Ninety-Eight and Delta Series Cars)

Equipment	Class I	Class II	Class III
Trailer Type	Any	Any	All except Toronado
Tongue Load Limit (lbs)	to 200 lbs	200 to 350 lbs	350 to 600 lbs
Engine Requirement	350 V-8	455 V-8	455 V-8
Exhaust System	Std.	Std.	Std.
Engine Cooling	H.D. System Recommended	H.D. System Required	H.D. System Required
Transmission Requirement	Turbo-Hydra-Matic 400 Recommended	Turbo-Hydra-Matic 400 Required	Turbo-Hydra-Matic 400 Required
Trans. Aux. Oil Cooler	Recommended	Required	Required
Axle Ratio Recommended	Std.	2.93:1 Required Except Toronado 3.07:1	2.93:1 Required
Differential Type	Anti-Spin is Available		
Wheels Recommended	Std.	Std.	Std.
Tires	Fiberglass Belted units Available	Fiberglass Belted units Recommended	Fiberglass Belted Required
Brakes Recommended	Std.	Std.	Std.
Front	Std.	Std.	Std.
Rear	Std.	Std.	Std.
Springs	H.D. Not Required	H.D. Recommended	H.D. Required
Shock Absorbers	H.D. units Available	H.D. units Recommended	H.D. units Required
Sway Bar	——	——	——
Steering Recommended	Std.	Std.	Std.
Battery Recommended	Std.	Std.	Std.
Alternator	Std.	Std.	Std.
Turn Signal Flasher	❋	❋	❋
Type Hitch Required	Frame	Equalizer	Equalizer

❋ An electrical harness for all units is recommended.

Trailer Towing Information

1969 Oldsmobile (Vista Cruiser, 4-4-2, Cutlass Supreme, Cutlass Series Cars)

Equipment	Class I	Class II	Class III ▲
Trailer Type	Any	Any	——
Tongue Load Limit (lbs)	to 200 lbs	200 to 350 lbs	——
Engine Requirement	350 V-8 or 400 V-8	350 V-8 or 400 V-8	——
Exhaust System	Std.	Std.	——
Engine Cooling	H.D. System Recommended	H.D. System Required	——
Transmission Requirement	Turbo-Hydra-Matic 350 Required	Turbo-Hydra-Matic 400 Required	——
Trans. Aux. Oil Cooler	Recommended	Required	——
Axle Ratio Recommended	3.08:1 Required	3.08:1 Required	——
Differential Type	Anti-Spin Axle-Available	Anti-Spin Axle-Available	——
Wheels Recommended	Std.	Std.	——
Tires	Fiberglass Belted Available	Fiberglass Belted Required	——
Brakes Recommended	Std.	Std.	——
Front	Std.	Std.	——
Rear	Std.	Std.	——
Springs	H.D. units Recommended	H.D. units Required	——
Shock Absorbers	H.D. units Recommended	H.D. units Required	——
Sway Bar	——	——	——
Steering Recommended	Std.	Std.	——
Battery Recommended	Std.	Std.	——
Alternator	Std.	Std.	——
Turn Signal Flasher	❂	❂	——
Type Hitch Required	Frame	Equalizing	——

❂ A trailer electrical package is recommended.
▲ It is not recommended that these cars tow Class III trailers.

1972 Trailer Towing Information

Pontiac (Full Size)

Equipment	Class I ●	Class II	Class III
Trailer Type	Any	Any	Any
Tongue Load Limit (lbs)	200	350	600
Engine Requirement	Std.①	400 cu in. V-8①	400 cu in. V-8①
Exhaust System	Std.	Std.②	Std.②
Engine Cooling	H.D.	H.D.	H.D.
Transmission Requirement	Std.	H.D.	H.D.
Trans. Aux. Oil Cooler	——	Yes	Yes
Axle Ratio Recommended	Std.	3.08:1	3.21:1
Differential Type	Std.	Std.	Std.
Wheels Recommended	H.D. 15 x 6	H.D. 15 x 6	H.D. 15 x 6
Tires	Std.	H78 x 15D③	H78 x 15D③
Brakes Recommended	Std.	Std.	Std.
Front	Std.	Std.	Std.
Rear	Std.	Std.	Std.
Springs	Std.	H.D.	H.D.④
Shock Absorbers	Std.	H.D.	H.D.
Sway Bar	——	——	——
Steering Recommended	Std.	Std.	Std.
Battery Recommended	Std.	Std.	Std.
Alternator	Std.	Std.	Std.
Turn Signal Flasher	H.D.	H.D.	H.D.
Type Hitch Required	Frame	Equalizer	Equalizer

● Firebird and Ventura can not tow a trailer over 1,000 lbs or 100 lbs tongue weight.
① Special spark plugs.
② Dual exhaust on 455 cu in. V-8 and 400 cu in. V-8 with 4 bbl. except Safaris.
③ L78 x 15D on Safaris.
④ H.D. frame.

1972 Trailer Towing Information

Le Mans and GTO

Equipment	Class I	Class II	Class III
Trailer Type	Any	Any	③
Tongue Load Limit (lbs)	200	350	③
Engine Requirement	350 cu in. V-8	350 cu in. V-8	③
Exhaust System	Std.	Std.	③
Engine Cooling	H.D.	H.D.	③
Transmission Requirement	Turbo-Hydra-Matic	Turbo-Hydra-Matic	③
Trans. Aux. Oil Cooler	——	——	③
Axle Ratio Recommended	Std.	Std.	③
Differential Type	Std.	Std.	③
Wheels Recommended	Std.	Std.	③
Tires	G78 x 14D①	G78 x 14D①	③
Brakes Recommended	Power	Power	③
Front	Std.	Std.	③
Rear	Std.	Std.	③
Springs	H.D.②	H.D.②	③
Shock Absorbers	H.D.	H.D.	③
Sway Bar	——	——	③
Steering Recommended	Std.	Std.	③
Battery Recommended	Std.	Std.	③
Alternator	Std.	Std.	③
Turn Signal Flasher	H.D.	H.D.	③
Type Hitch Required	Frame	Equalizer	③

① H78 x 14B on Wagons.
② H.D. Frame.
③ Vehicle is not recommended to tow a Class III trailer.

1972 Trailer Towing Information

Grand Prix

Equipment	Class I	Class II	Class III
Trailer Type	Any	Any	①
Tongue Load Limit (lbs)	200	350	①
Engine Requirement	400 cu in. V-8	400 cu in. V-8	①
Exhaust System	Std.	Std.	①
Engine Cooling	H.D.	H.D.	①
Transmission Requirement	Std.	Std.	①
Trans. Aux. Oil Cooler	——	——	①
Axle Ratio Recommended	Std.	Std.	①
Differential Type	Std.	Std.	①
Wheels Recommended	Std.	Std.	①
Tires	G78 x 14D	G78 x 14D	①
Brakes Recommended	Std.	Std.	①
Front	Std.	Std.	①
Rear	Std.	Std.	①
Springs	H.D.	H.D.	①
Shock Absorbers	H.D.	H.D.	①
Sway Bar	——	——	①
Steering Recommended	Std.	Std.	①
Battery Recommended	Std.	Std.	①
Alternator	Std.	Std.	①
Turn Signal Flasher	H.D.	H.D.	①
Type Hitch Required	Frame	Equalizer	①

① It is not recommended that Grand Prix tow Class III trailers.

1971 Trailer Towing Information

Pontiac except Grand Prix and Le Mans

Equipment	Class I	Class II	Class III
Trailer Type	Any	Any	Any
Tongue Load Limit (lbs)	200	350	600
Engine Requirement	Std.②	Std.②	Std.②
Exhaust System	Std.	Std.①	Std.①
Engine Cooling	H.D.	H.D.	H.D.
Transmission Requirement		H.D. Turbo Hydro	
Trans. Aux. Oil Cooler	——	Yes	Yes
Axle Ratio Recommended	3.08:1	3.08:1	3.23:1
Differential Type	Std.	Std.	Std.
Wheels Recommended	H.D.	H.D.	H.D.
Tires	Std.	H78 x 15D③	H78 x 15D③
Brakes Recommended	Std.	Std.	Std.
Front	Std.	Std.	Std.
Rear	Std.	Std.	Std.
Springs	Std.	H.D.	H.D.
Shock Absorbers	Std.	H.D.	H.D.
Sway Bar	——	——	——
Steering Recommended	Std.	Std.	Std.
Battery Recommended	Std.	Std.	Std.
Alternator	Std.	Std.	Std.
Turn Signal Flasher	H.D.	H.D.	H.D.
Type Hitch Required	Frame	Equalizer	Equalizer

① Dual Exhaust with 455 cu in. and 400 cu in. 4 bbl.
② Special spark plugs.
③ L78 x 15D on wagons.

1971 Trailer Towing Information

Grand Prix

Equipment	Class I	Class II	Class III
Trailer Type	Any	Any	①
Tongue Load Limit (lbs)	200	350	①
Engine Requirement	Std.	Std.	①
Exhaust System	Std.	Std.	①
Engine Cooling	H.D.	H.D.	①
Transmission Requirement	Std.	Std.	①
Trans. Aux. Oil Cooler	——	——	①
Axle Ratio Recommended	3.23:1	3.23:1	①
Differential Type	Std.	Std.	①
Wheels Recommended	Std.	Std.	①
Tires	G78 x 14D	G78 x 14D	①
Brakes Recommended	Std.	Std.	①
Front	Std.	Std.	①
Rear	Std.	Std.	①
Springs	H.D.	H.D.	①
Shock Absorbers	H.D.	H.D.	①
Sway Bar	——	——	①
Steering Recommended	Std.	Std.	①
Battery Recommended	Std.	Std.	①
Alternator	Std.	Std.	①
Turn Signal Flasher	H.D.	H.D.	①
Type Hitch Required	Frame	Equalizer	①

① It is not recommended that Grand Prix tow Class III trailers.

1971 Trailer Towing Information

Le Mans, GTO

Equipment	Class I	Class II	Class III
Trailer Type	Any	Any	③
Tongue Load Limit (lbs)	200	350	③
Engine Requirement	Std.	Std.	③
Exhaust System	Std.	Std.	③
Engine Cooling	H.D.	H.D.	③
Transmission Requirement	Std.	Std.	③
Trans. Aux. Oil Cooler	——	——	③
Axle Ratio Recommended	3.55:1	3.55:1	③
Differential Type	Std.	Std.	③
Wheels Recommended	Std.	Std.	③
Tires	G78 x 14D①	G78 x 14D①	③
Brakes Recommended	Power	Power	③
Front	Std.	Std.	③
Rear	Std.	Std.	③
Springs	H.D.②	H.D.②	③
Shock Absorbers	H.D.	H.D.	③
Sway Bar	——	——	③
Steering Recommended	Std.	Std.	③
Battery Recommended	Std.	Std.	③
Alternator	Std.	Std.	③
Turn Signal Flasher	H.D.	H.D.	③
Type Hitch Required	Frame	Equalizer	③

① H78 x 14B on wagons.
② H.D. frame.
③ Vehicle is not recommended to tow Class III trailers.

Trailer Towing Information

1970 Pontiac (Tempest, Le Mans, Le Mans Sport, GTO)

Equipment	Class I	Class II	Class III ▲
Trailer Type	Any	Any	——
Tongue Load Limit (lbs)	up to 200 lbs	200 to 350 lbs	——
Engine Requirement	Std.	Std.	——
Exhaust System	Std.	Std.	——
Engine Cooling	H.D. System & Flex Fan	H.D. System & Flex Fan	——
Transmission Requirement	Man. or Auto.	Man. or Auto.	——
Trans. Aux. Oil Cooler	Not Required	Not Required	——
Axle Ratio Recommended	3.55:1 Auto. 3.55:1 Man.	3.55:1 Auto. 3.55:1 Man.	——
Differential Type	Std.	Std.	——
Wheels Recommended	Std.	Std.	——
Tires	G78-14 Range D H78-14 Range B (Station Wagons)	G78-14 Range D H-78-14 Range B (Station Wagons)	——
Brakes Recommended	Std.	Std.	——
Front	Std.	Std.	——
Rear	Std.	Std.	——
Springs	H.D.	H.D.	——
Shock Absorbers	H.D.	H.D.	——
Sway Bar	N.A.	N.A.	——
Steering Recommended	Std.	Std.	——
Battery Recommended	Std.	Std.	——
Alternator	Std.	Std.	——
Turn Signal Flasher	Std.	Std.	——
Type Hitch Required	Frame	Equalizer Type	——

H.D.—Heavy Duty
Man.—Manual
Auto.—Automatic
Note: A special trailer-hauling package is available for all classes. It includes:
1. A constant rate directional flasher.
2. A special wiring harness.
3. Special spark plugs and heavy-duty wheels.
▲ Towing Class III trailers not recommended.

Trailer Towing Information

1970 Pontiac (Grand Prix)

Equipment	Class I	Class II	Class III ▲
Trailer Type	Any	Any	——
Tongue Load Limit (lbs)	up to 200 lbs	200 to 350 lbs	——
Engine Requirement	Std.	Std.	——
Exhaust System	Std.	Std.	——
Engine Cooling	H.D. System w/ Flex-Fan	H.D. System w/ Flex-Fan	——
Transmission Requirement	Std.	Std.	——
Trans. Aux. Oil Cooler	Not Required	Not Required	——
Axle Ratio Recommended	3.23:1 Auto. 3.23:1 Manual	3.23:1 Auto. 3.23:1 Manual	——
Differential Type	Std.	Std.	——
Wheels Recommended	Std.	Std.	——
Tires	G78-14 Range D	G78-14 Range D	——
Brakes Recommended	Std.	Std.	——
Front	Std.	Std.	——
Rear	Std.	Std.	——
Springs	H.D.	H.D.	——
Shock Absorbers	H.D.	H.D.	——
Sway Bar	——	——	——
Steering Recommended	Std.	Std.	——
Battery Recommended	Std.	Std.	——
Alternator	Std.	Std.	——
Turn Signal Flasher	Std.	Std.	——
Type Hitch Required	Frame	Equalizer Type	——

H.D.—Heavy Duty.
Man.—Manual.
Auto.—Automatic.
Note: A special trailer-hauling package is available for all classes. It includes:
1. A constant rate directional flasher.
2. A special wiring harness.
3. Special spark plugs and heavy-duty wheels.
▲ Towing Class III trailers not recommended.

Trailer Towing Information

Equipment	Class I	Class II	Class III
Trailer Type	Any	Any	Any
Tongue Load Limit (lbs)	up to 200 lbs	200 to 350 lbs	350 to 600 lbs
Engine Requirement	Std.	Std.	Std.
Exhaust System	Standard	Dual	Dual
Engine Cooling	H.D. System w/ Flex Fan		
Transmission Requirement	Man. or Auto.	Man. or Auto. H.D. Turbo Hydromatic	Man. or Auto. H.D. Turbo Hydromatic
Trans. Aux. Oil Cooler	Not Required	Required	Required
Axle Ratio Recommended	2.93:1 Auto. 3.42:1 Manual	2.93:1 Auto. 3.42:1 Manual	2.93:1 Auto. 3.42:1 Manual
Differential Type	Std.	Std.	Std.
Wheels Recommended	H.D.	H.D.	H.D.
Tires	Std.	H78-15 Load Range D L78-15 or 9.15-15 on Station Wagons	H78-15 Load Range D L78-15 or 9.15-15 on Station Wagons
Brakes Recommended	Std.	Std.	Std.
Front	Std.	Std.	Std.
Rear	Std.	Std.	Std.
Springs	Std.	H.D.	H.D.
Shock Absorbers	Std.	H.D.	H.D.
Sway Bar	N.A.	N.A.	N.A.
Steering Recommended	Std.	Std.	Std.
Battery Recommended	Std.	Std.	Std.
Alternator	Std.	Std.	Std.
Turn Signal Flasher	Constant Rate Flasher		
Type Hitch Required	Frame	Frame	H.D. Frame

H.D.—Heavy Duty
Note: A special trailer-hauling package is available for all classes. It includes:
1. A constant rate directional flasher.
2. A special wiring harness.
3. Special spark plugs and heavy-duty wheels.

Trailer Towing Information

1969 Pontiac (Tempest, Custom S, Le Mans, Le Mans Safari, GTO)

Equipment	Class I	Class II	Class III
Trailer Type	Any	—	—
Tongue Load Limit (lbs)	up to 200 lbs	—	—
Engine Requirement	Std.	—	—
Exhaust System	Std.	—	—
Engine Cooling	H.D. System w/ Flex Fan	—	—
Transmission Requirement	Man. or Auto.	—	—
Trans. Aux. Oil Cooler	Not Required	—	—
Axle Ratio Recommended	3.55:1 OHC 6 3.36:1 350 V-8	—	—
Differential Type	Std.	—	—
Wheels Recommended	Std.	—	—
Tires	8.25-14	—	—
Brakes Recommended	Std.	—	—
Front	Std.	—	—
Rear	Std.	—	—
Springs	H.D.	—	—
Shock Absorbers	H.D.	—	—
Sway Bar	—	—	—
Steering Recommended	Std.	—	—
Battery Recommended	Std.	—	—
Alternator	Std.	—	—
Turn Signal Flasher	Constant Rate Flasher	—	—
Type Hitch Required	Frame	—	—

H.D.—Heavy Duty

Note: A special trailer-hauling package is available for all classes. It includes:
1. A constant rate directional flasher.
2. A special wiring harness.
3. Special spark plugs and heavy-duty wheels.

Trailer Towing Information

1969 Pontiac (Grand Prix)

Equipment	Class I	Class II	Class III
Trailer Type	Any	—	—
Tongue Load Limit (lbs)	up to 200 lbs	—	—
Engine Requirement	400 cu in. V-8	—	—
Exhaust System	Std.	—	—
Engine Cooling	H.D. System w/ Flex Fan	—	—
Transmission Requirement	Turbo-Hydra-Matic	—	—
Trans. Aux. Oil Cooler	Not Required	—	—
Axle Ratio Recommended	Std.	—	—
Differential Type	Std.	—	—
Wheels Recommended	Std.	—	—
Tires	Std.	—	—
Brakes Recommended	Std.	—	—
Front	Std.	—	—
Rear	Std.	—	—
Springs	H.D.	—	—
Shock Absorbers	H.D.	—	—
Sway Bar	—	—	—
Steering Recommended	Std.	—	—
Battery Recommended	Std.	—	—
Alternator	Std.	—	—
Turn Signal Flasher	Contant Rate Flasher	—	—
Type Hitch Required	Frame	—	—

H.D.—Heavy Duty
Note: A special trailer-hauling package is available for all classes. It includes:
1. A constant rate directional flasher.
2. A special wiring harness.
3. Special spark plugs and heavy-duty wheels.

Trailer Towing Information

1969 Pontiac (Catalina, Executive, Bonneville)

Equipment	Class I	Class II	Class III
Trailer Type	Any	Any	Any
Tongue Load Limit (lbs)	up to 200 lbs	200 to 350 lbs	350 to 600 lbs
Engine Requirement	Std.	Std.	Std.
Exhaust System	Std.	Std.	Std.
Engine Cooling		H.D. System w/ Flex Fan	
Transmission Requirement	Man. or Auto.	Auto. (Turbo-Hydra-Matic)	Auto. (Turbo-Hydra-Matic)
Trans. Aux. Oil Cooler	Not Required	Required	Required
Axle Ratio Recommended	2.93:1 Catalina & Executive 3.08:1 Bonneville	3.08:1 All Models	3.23:1 All Models
Differential Type	Std.	Std.	Std.
Wheels Recommended	Std.	Std.	Std.
Tires	Std.	8.85-15	8.85-15
Brakes Recommended	Std.	Std.	Std.
Front	Std.	Std.	Std.
Rear	Std.	Std.	Std.
Springs	Std.	H.D.	H.D.
Shock Absorbers	Std.	H.D.	H.D.
Sway Bar	——	——	——
Steering Recommended	Std.	Std.	Std.
Battery Recommended	Std.	Std.	Std.
Alternator	Std.	Std.	Std.
Turn Signal Flasher		Constant Rate Flasher	
Type Hitch Required	Frame	Frame	H.D. Frame

H.D.—Heavy Duty
Note: A special trailer-hauling package is available for all classes. It includes:
1. A constant rate directional flasher.
2. A special wiring harness.
3. Special spark plugs and heavy-duty wheels.

Trailer Towing Information

1968 Pontiac (Tempest, Tempest Custom, Tempest Safari, Le Mans, GTO)

Equipment	Class I	Class II	Class III
Trailer Type	Any	——	——
Tongue Load Limit (lbs)	up to 200 lbs	——	——
Engine Requirement	Std.	——	——
Exhaust System	Std.	——	——
Engine Cooling	H.D. System w/ H.D. Fan	——	——
Transmission Requirement	Man. & Auto.	——	——
Trans. Aux. Oil Cooler	Not Required	——	——
Axle Ratio Recommended	3.55:1 w/ OHC 6 cyl. 3.36:1 w/ 350 V-8	——	——
Differential Type	Std.	——	——
Wheels Recommended	Std.	——	——
Tires	Std.	——	——
Brakes Recommended	Std.	——	——
Front	Std.	——	——
Rear	Std.	——	——
Springs	H.D.	——	——
Shock Absorbers	H.D.	——	——
Sway Bar	——	——	——
Steering Recommended	Std.	——	——
Battery Recommended	Std.	——	——
Alternator	Std.	——	——
Turn Signal Flasher	Constant Rate Flasher	——	——
Type Hitch Required	Frame	——	——

H.D.—Heavy Duty
Note: A special trailer-hauling package is available for all classes. It includes:
1. A constant rate directional flasher.
2. A special wiring harness.
3. Special spark plugs and heavy-duty wheels.

Trailer Towing Information

1968 Pontiac (Catalina, Executive, Bonneville, Grand Prix)

Equipment	Class I	Class II	Class III
Trailer Type	Any	Any	Any
Tongue Load Limit (lbs)	up to 200 lbs	200 to 350 lbs	350 to 600 lbs
Engine Requirement	Std.	Std.	Std.
Exhaust System	Std.	Std.	Std.
Engine Cooling		H.D. w/ H.D. Fan	
Transmission Requirement		Man. or Auto. (Turbo-Hydra-Matic)	
Trans. Aux. Oil Cooler	Not Required	Required	Required
Axle Ratio Recommended	2.93:1 w/ Turbo-Hydra-Matic	3.08:1 w/ H.D. Turbo-Hydra-Matic	3.23:1 w/ H.D. Turbo-Hydra-Matic
Differential Type	Std.	Std.	Std.
Wheels Recommended	Std.	Std.	Std.
Tires	Std.	Std.	Std.
Brakes Recommended	Std.	Std.	Std.
Front	Std.	Std.	Std.
Rear	Std.	Std.	Std.
Springs	Std.	H.D.	H.D.
Shock Absorbers	Std.	H.D.	H.D.
Sway Bar	——	——	——
Steering Recommended	Std.	Std.	Std.
Battery Recommended	Std.	Std.	Std.
Alternator	Std.	Std.	Std.
Turn Signal Flasher		Constant Rate Flasher	
Type Hitch Required	Frame	Equalizer	Equalizer

H.D.—Heavy Duty
Note: A special trailer-hauling package is available for all classes. It includes:
1. A constant rate directional flasher.
2. A special wiring harness.
3. Special spark plugs and heavy-duty wheels.

3 · Water and Sewage

The Water System

The water system of the average camper trailer can vary from a water holding tank with a hand pump faucet to an automatic faucet with an electric water pump that matches the efficiency of a home unit.

The manual that you can obtain from your dealer contains the water system for your particular trailer. It is important to note the location of the holding tank, electric pump (if so equipped), and the plumbing. This will save time if a malfunction arises.

THE WATER PUMP

There are two types of pumping mechanisms in the average trailer: the electric pump, and the self-priming manual pump.

The electric pump is fastened in an inline connection between the fresh water holding tank and the faucet. Turning on the faucet energizes a switch inside the faucet which sends current to the electric pump unit. The pump is activated and circulates the water until the pump switch is de-energized by turning off the faucet.

The manual pump works on the power principle; the harder you pump, the more water you get. The plunger in the pump creates a limited vacuum which sucks the water from the holding tank through the faucet.

Water Pump Removal

To remove the water pump from the trailer, use the following procedures.

1. Turn off the water supply and the pump switch.
2. Remove the electrical input to the pump.
3. Remove the input and output hoses to the pump, being certain to tag them before removal.
4. Loosen and remove the pump attaching screws and remove the pump from the trailer.
5. Replacement is accomplished by reversing the above procedure.

Operation

To prime the system, perform the following steps.

1. Fill the fresh water holding tank, making sure all the drain valves are closed.
2. Energize the main current to the pump.
3. Keep all outlets open until water appears.
4. Close the outlet and de-energize the pump (if the pump is equipped with a manual energizer switch).

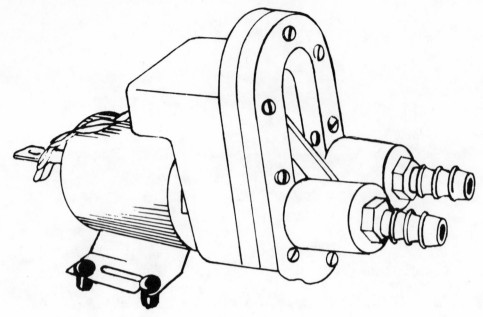

An electric water pump

NOTE: *Since there are large iron and lime deposits in some parts of the country, it is a good idea to flush the water tank frequently. Mix a cleaning solution of bicarbonate of soda and water ($\frac{1}{4}$–$\frac{1}{2}$ lbs of soda), pour it into the tank, and allow it to settle there. Rinse the tank clean and refill it with drinking water.*

Water Pump Troubleshooting Chart

Condition	Remedy
1. Pump runs but there is no pressure	1. Check the water level in the holding tank.
	2. Make certain that the electrical power is sufficient.
	3. See that all the required valves are open.
	4. Check for leaks.
	5. Check for suction at the pump. If there is none, the pump must be repaired or replaced.
2. Noise in the pump	1. Examine the pump mounting bolts for looseness.
	2. Make certain that both inlet and outlet hoses are clear and properly installed.
	3. If the faucet has an aerator, remove it and check for blockage.
3. Pump does not run	1. Check the electrical connections for contact.
	2. Check the amount of current to the pump motor.
	3. Examine the pump for defects.

WATER HEATER

Water heaters are usually not included in the average camper trailer, although they are offered, as an option, on some models. The heater serves as one more means of bringing the comforts of home with you while you are away from home.

There are two basic types of water heater; gas and electric. The gas type heats the water by means of a flame encompassing the cold water coils; the electric heats by transferring heat to electric coils which surround the water jackets. There must be no air in either system, so run water from all the hot water faucets until it runs smoothly.

Gas-operated heaters work on the same principle as do gas-operated refrigerators. (See "Refrigerator.") They utilize a thermocouple. Use the same procedure for starting the pilot as was used to start the pilot on the refrigerator.

Since the heater's operation is similar to that of the gas-operated refrigerator, it will have approximately the same malfunctions. If the heater does not operate, check the obvious causes first. It is usually something simple; either the gas has run out or the pilot has blown out or something similar. Malfunctions in the electric system are few although the most frequent are shorted or loose wires. Any other problem with either type of heater should be serviced by qualified personnel only.

NOTE: *There have been cases in which a low, off-colored flame has been produced in gas units by an obstruction in the air supply tube. This tube is located just ahead of the burner. Remove the obstruction with compressed air.*

Gas-type water heater

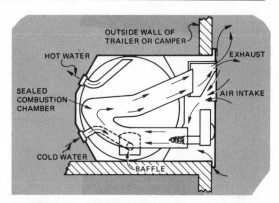

Internal diagram of the water heater

Whenever the unit is to be stored (especially during below-freezing temperatures), drain the water heater by opening the faucets and then opening the drain valve on the outside of the trailer. Allow the system to drain completely before closing the drain valves and faucets.

The Sewage System

The sewage system of the average camper trailer consists of the toilet assembly, the plumbing, and the holding tank assembly. Because of size, the plumbing system is not as complicated as in a travel trailer which usually offers all the modern facilities found at home.

Any trouble can be prevented with only routine maintenance of the sewage system. Consult the owner's manual for your camper to find the exact location of the sewage plumbing and the access holes in the chassis for maintenance. Also be familiar with the capacity of the tank and the chemicals acceptable for cleaning and deodorizing the holding tank. Use the prescribed chemicals at the appropriate intervals to keep the system trouble-free.

TOILET ASSEMBLY

There are three basic types of toilets presently used in campers: the fresh water type; recirculating type; and the portable type.

The fresh water type works, as the name indicates, from the fresh water holding tank. Every time the unit is used, a new supply of water is circulated through the

Fresh water type toilet

Portable toilets are most common on the smaller camper trailers and consist of a unit which can be moved from one place to another. They are totally self-contained. These units consist of the toilet assembly with two separate tanks. One tank contains fresh water while the other acts as the holding tank into which the chemicals are added.

Portable type toilet

toilet by the pump and is transferred to the holding tank with the waste.

The recirculating type toilet was adapted from aircraft to trailers. This is a completely independent type which is powered by an electric motor. There is a storage facility inside the tank for approximately eight gallons of fluid. It is filled with four gallons of water and the added chemicals and is good for about 80–100 uses. On trailers equipped with a holding tank, the toilet may be drained into the tank and the toilet may be refilled for continued use.

This type of unit usually has two foot controls: one lever to open the holding tank valve which will allow the entrance of the waste from the bowl; and the pump lever which will allow the entrance of the waste into the toilet bowl. Most of the units include a detachable waste tank which can be removed for disposal.

The portable types are truly movable with limited effort. Because of this and their ease of maintenance they are most popular in the smaller trailers where the owner does not truly want to "rough it."

Recirculating type toilet

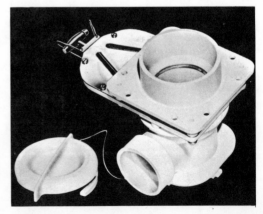

Waste valve

Operation of a Recirculating Type Toilet

PREPARATION FOR USE

Generally these units are primed with approximately 4–5 gal. of water. Check the operating instructions obtained with the unit. There is an apparent change in the noise level of the water when flushing some units. This means that the water has reached its capacity.

Once the water is added, flush the toilet and add the necessary chemicals. The manufacturer of the system will state the type of chemicals to be used and the intervals at which they are to be added. Once the chemicals are added, flush through about five cycles to ensure thorough mixing of the chemicals and water. The unit is now ready for use.

The newly charged system is capable of about 80 usages or approximately 5 days. It is recommended that the system be cleaned after each trip. The unit is full when the fluid level becomes evident at the bottom of the bowl.

If the unit is used in below-freezing temperatures, add antifreeze to the initial charge. Some manufacturers recommend that only ethylene base antifreeze be used. Check with the manufacturer's literature for the recommended antifreeze to be used before experimenting.

Emptying the System

If the trailer is equipped with a holding tank, a direct line can be connected from the toilet to the holding tank to allow the toilet to be drained at will.

If there is no holding tank available, connect a hose to the drainage duct at the base of the toilet and open the discharge valve slowly to release the waste. Only discharge at a certified disposal station. Once waste is discharged, fill the unit with 4–6 gal water and ½ cup of toilet cleaner. Allow the mixture to sit overnight for best results. Drain and flush the unit with clean water before recharging it.

Winterizing the System

Drain the input line to the toilet assembly and then, by pumping the foot pedal of the toilet, remove all the water from the system. It is important to remove *all* water; freezing will cause expansion and damage the plumbing.

The waste holding tank should be cleaned, rinsed, drained and then blown dry with compressed air, if possible. Once the system is cleaned and drained, the addition of some chemicals is recommended to prevent rust and other harmful effects of low temperatures. Consult your owner's manual for manufacturer's recommendations.

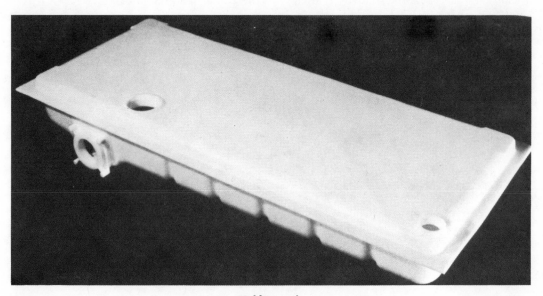

Holding tank

If the camper is to be used during the winter, the system must be protected from freezing. There are a great number of commercial antifreeze additives but consult your dealer for his recommendations first.

WATER TANK REMOVAL

Because of the various locations of water tanks, the procedure listed below is a general procedure which can be adapted for each specific model.

1. Drain the water tank completely.
2. Remove the connections from the inlet and outlet hoses and also the vent hose.
3. Make sure all the connections to the tank are removed (including the electrical connections if they are present).
4. Remove the tank shielding from the underside of the tank if so equipped.
5. Loosen and remove the tank supports while bracing the tank assembly from the bottom.
6. Remove the tank from the chassis.
7. Installation may be accomplished by reversing the removal procedure.

NOTE: *Any insulating material which is removed must be replaced when the tank is reinstalled.*

HOLDING TANK

Holding tank capacities vary in size from camper to camper but usually range from 15 to 25 gal. The size usually depends on the type of system used in the camper. Generally there are three types of drainage system used: the single-tank; two-tank; and the by-pass holding tank systems.

The single-tank system is the type where all the drainage outlets empty into one holding tank. Of course this necessitates the use of a larger holding tank than the others. The two-tank system provides a separate tank which is directly connected to the toilet while another tank holds the waste from the shower and sink. The by-pass system consists of a holding tank for the toilet waste while all other waste is channeled from the camper either through a sewer line or a catch receptacle.

Emptying the Holding Tank

NOTE: *It is of paramount importance that the holding tank of any camper be emptied* only *at an approved disposal site. There are severe penalties imposed by the government for violators.*

The tank can be drained by fastening the discharge hose from the trailer to the fitting on the sewer opening. Make certain that both the connection of the hose at the trailer and at the sewer are made securely as there will be a great amount of pressure flowing through the waste line. The tank should be washed out with clean water once it has been drained. Also wash the inside of the drain hose. As a final measure, add the chemicals recommended by the trailer manufacturer.

4 · Fuel and Heating

The Liquid Petroleum Gas System

The liquid petroleum gas (LPG) system is used in most camper trailers for heating, cooking, lighting, and refrigeration. This system affords the mobility and convenience of bottled gas.

The gas is usually stored in pressure containers which are generally mounted on the tongue assembly and is fed from there into the trailer chassis. The gas lines are usually ½ in. copper tubing with brass connectors, or possibly sweat fittings on the older models. The gas feeds the different appliances in the trailer through these lines.

TYPES OF FUEL

Butane and propane are the two basic fuels for all trailers, and camper trailers in particular. Both produce a clean, even flame which is ideal for cooking and heating.

Both gases can be stored in a closed container and can be converted by pressure from a liquid to a gas which are valuable assets. The gas remains at the top inside the container while the liquid gas is on the bottom. As the gas at the top is

LP gas container

used, the reduction in the pressure within the cylinder causes the vaporization of the liquid in the bottom and this converts it to gas. The container is empty when all the liquid gas has vaporized and all the upper gas has been used.

It has been proven that a gallon of butane produces more heat than a gallon of propane. Butane, however, has a higher

99

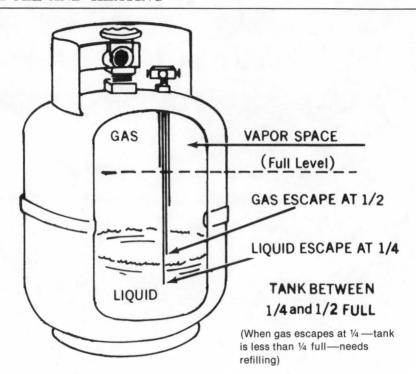

GAS

VAPOR SPACE

(Full Level)

GAS ESCAPE AT 1/2

LIQUID ESCAPE AT 1/4

LIQUID

TANK BETWEEN 1/4 and 1/2 FULL

(When gas escapes at ¼—tank is less than ¼ full—needs refilling)

LP cylinder internal components with gas escape levels

"freezing" point than propane. "Freezing" means that the evaporization quality by which it turns from a liquid to a gas is stopped and it remains as a liquid. Consequently, butane cannot be used where the temperature is below 32° F. Propane, since it does have a lower freezing temperature, is sometimes mixed with butane to lower the overall freezing temperature. Propane can also be used alone, especially where the climate is extremely cold.

The size of the bottled-gas tank and the degree of heating done with gas will regulate the life of the gas tank. Do not allow the tank to empty, since air will enter the gas lines, causing them to be bled before the system can be reused.

It is possible to fit the tank with a gauge on some units. This will make it possible to tell exactly how much gas the cylinder contains. The weight of the tank compared to a full cylinder is the easiest way of measuring, but it is also possible to note the condensation marks on the outside of the container; these mark the upper level of the gas.

TRAILER GAS FLOOR PLAN

Some gas line connections may come loose and can cause a gas leak due to road

LP gas gauge (© Airstream Corp.)

vibrations. It is, therefore, necessary to know the floor plan of the system and the location of the fittings and connections so they will be easily accessible for a check.

The floor plan for the LPG system should be found in the owner's manual for the trailer. If not, your dealer's service manual should include the information. If

GAS DISTRIBUTION SYSTEM L.Y. 21 FT.

1. Flexible connector
2. Union elbow no. 55
3. Tubing, copper ⅝" O.D.
4. ⅝ x ⅝ x ⅜ tee
5. Furnace
6. Tubing, copper ⅜" O.D.
7. Water heater
8. ⅜ x ⅝ x ⅜ tee
9. Range
10. ⅜ x ⅜ x ¼ tee
11. Tubing, copper ¼" O.D.
12. Refrigerator
13. L.P.G. light

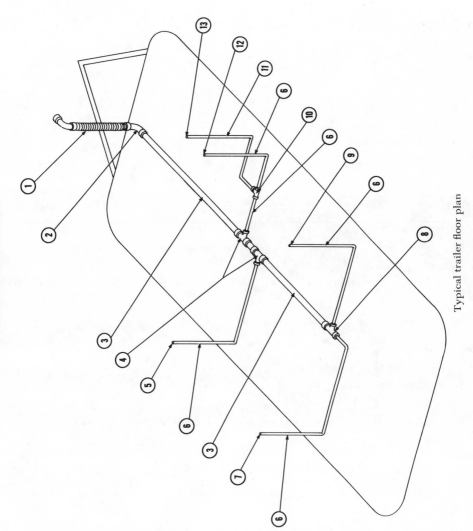

Typical trailer floor plan

your trailer is second-hand, see the dealer for that particular brand to get the needed information. The only other means of learning the layout of the LPG system is to find out yourself. Trace the lines through the trailer to the various appliances. This may be a hard and time-consuming job, but it is necessary to avoid leaks which can cause explosions.

GAS RACK ASSEMBLY

The bottled gas rack assembly is a welded or bolted unit attached to the tongue of the trailer. It houses and supports the bottled gas tanks and the regulator system. The rack is usually composed of a level plate which stretches across the two tongue beams. A stationary center bar extends up from the middle of the rack plate on double-tank models.

The LPG gas tank(s) is inserted into the bottom plate of the rack which usually has a rim around the edge to keep the gas container from slipping off. Once the tank is centered, securely fasten it from the top so the container will not move when under tow.

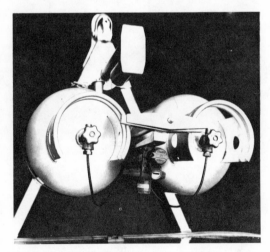

Gas rack assembly (© Airstream Corp.)

LPG TANK REMOVAL AND REPLACEMENT

1. Remove the regulator assembly from the tank(s).
2. Loosen and remove the upper support brace.
3. Remove the tank from the bottom holder.
4. The replacement procedure is the reverse of the removal.

LPG Regulator

The regulator on the bottled gas container is an important addition to the fuel system. The valve governs the amount of pressure that the gas appliances receive from the bottled gas container and once the regulator is adjusted at the factory, it should not be touched again. If the regulator is found to be faulty, a new unit should be installed and adjusted by a qualified person.

To remove the regulator from the tank system, close the open-close valves on the tank(s). Remove the connecting lines with the regulator attached and remove the regulator from the attachment line(s) by releasing the coupling.

Some systems use an automatic gas regulator which is attached to both tanks. While the on-off valves on both tanks are open all the time, the regulator draws from only one tank at a time. One tank is used until it is empty and then the regulator automatically switches to the full tank so the empty tank can be disconnected and refilled. The empty tank's valve is shut off so it can be removed and recharged. It is reinstalled by connecting the output line from the regulator to the tank and then opening the valve.

Testing the LPG System for Leaks

If there is evidence of a leak (sound or smell), testing procedures should begin im-

LP gas regulator (© Airstream Corp.)

mediately because the probability of a fire or explosion is great. Make frequent checks of the connections, fittings, and outlet valves to lessen the possibility of a leak.

Since LP gas is clear and odorless after it is refined, federal law requires that it be combined with Mercaptan which has a distinctive odor. If there is a leak, the Mercaptan should be evident and the degree of the odor will mark the seriousness of the leak. If there is a great amount of odor, the gas should be turned off at the tanks, all windows and doors of the trailer should be opened, and the trailer should be evacuated until the smell subsides. Mix a combination of soap and water in solution. This will be the leak finder. Never use a match or flame to find gas leaks. Once it is safe to enter the trailer, coat the suspected fittings with the solution, have an assistant turn on the gas, and watch for air bubbles at the fitting. Use this procedure at all of the suspected fittings.

The average gas line is ¾ in. tubing with flared fitting endings. Usually the problem lies with fittings which have come loose because of road vibration. Securely tightening the fitting should cure the leak. Do not overtighten the fitting or the flared end could be damaged beyond repair. All that is necessary in tightening is a snug fit. Never use any type of sealing compound on a flared fitting; this will only clog the line and distort the seating surface of the connector.

The procedure listed above is the best method of locating leaks. It is easier to locate small leaks if the gas is not entirely turned off at the tank. If you still can't find the leak after testing all the connections along the route of the gas line and determining that the lines are secure and not bent, turn off the gas and take your trailer to a service center.

Heating System

OPERATION

A heater of some type is a necessity for year-round camping in colder climates. Those heaters available for camper trailers (usually as an option) are small units con-

Camper trailer heater

structed as an integral part of the lower cabinet assembly.

The procedure by which heaters heat varies only slightly from model to model. The air which is to be combined with the gas is drawn from the outside of the camper through an air intake and into the sealer burner chamber. This air is next combined with the gas at the venturi port where combustion takes place. The heat from the main and pilot burners is vented to the outside through the combustion vent. As explained, most units have a sealed combustion system which prevents the products of combustion from entering the living area.

Once the heat is produced by combustion, it must be distributed throughout the camper to be effective. This is accomplished by the air circulation system. (See "Blower Assembly.") An internal fan moves cooler air from the interior of the camper across the surfaces of the heat exchanger which warms the air. This air is then channeled out of the heating ducts and into the trailer. There is usually a filtering device at the air intake to free the trailer air of dust and dirt particles.

THE PILOT

Most heaters work by means of a thermocouple. To light the unit, it is usually necessary to depress a button (red) and light the pilot with an extension wick while keeping the button depressed until

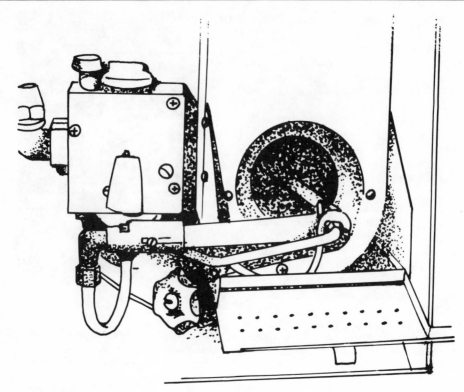

Heater pilot assembly

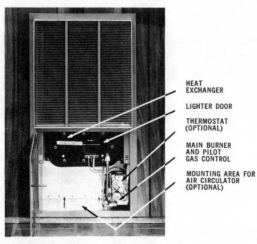

HEAT
EXCHANGER

LIGHTER DOOR

THERMOSTAT
(OPTIONAL)

MAIN BURNER
AND PILOT
GAS CONTROL

MOUNTING AREA FOR
AIR CIRCULATOR
(OPTIONAL)

Heater internal components

air screw is the only means of adjustment. Turning the screw clockwise usually increases the air which leans the flame; turning the screw counterclockwise lowers the air supply and richens the flame. If there is too much air, there will be a howling noise when the burner is working. A rich flame situation is evidenced by sooting in the vent and a yellow burner flame.

BLOWER ASSEMBLY

The blower assembly is situated inside the heating unit and circulates the inside trailer air over the heated coils to produce trailer heat. This is a completely closed system. There is no mixture of the burner gases which serve to heat the heating coils and the air which is moved by the blower around these coils to produce trailer heat.

When the thermostat indicates that heat is needed, the blower motor engages immediately. As the blower motor is in motion, the microswitch trips and channels gas to the main burner where it is lit by the pilot. Some units which have run for a long time have a tendency to keep the blower motor running even though the burner is in the "off" position. This re-

the unit will stay lit when the button is released.

GAS BURNER ADJUSTMENT

The burner is usually located behind a lower access panel. On some of the newer models it may be slightly harder to locate. If the pilot is out, light it and observe the color and intensity of the flame. The flame should be blue with a small yellow tip. An

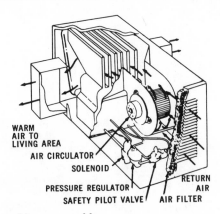

WARM
AIR TO
LIVING AREA

AIR CIRCULATOR

SOLENOID

RETURN
AIR

PRESSURE REGULATOR

SAFETY PILOT VALVE

AIR FILTER

Heater blower assembly

moves the remaining gases which may be trapped in the heat exchanger.

HEATER MAINTENANCE

If the burner is adjusted properly, the heater assembly should need no maintenance. A deposit of soot usually forms on the inside of the combustion chamber and must be removed before it causes blockage.

The best means of cleaning the combustion chamber is to lay either wet pieces of cloth or paper towels below the chamber to catch the soot as it falls. Use a soft brush or cloth to wipe the chamber clean. Some manufacturers recommend using a vacuum cleaner to suck the soot out but this may ruin the vacuum. Catch the soot or a coating of soot will fill the camper.

Heater Troubleshooting

Symptom	Remedy
1. No heat	1. Check to see if there is gas in the cylinder and also make certain that the supply valve is in the "on" position.
	2. Check to see that the pilot has not been blown out.
	3. Examine the electrical connections to the blower for a short or loose connection.
	4. Inspect the microswitch to see if it is functioning correctly. Clean all dirt deposits from the actuator pin.
	5. Examine the blower for a burned out motor.
2. Pilot will not stay lit	1. Check the thermocouple and replace it as necessary.
	2. Check for air leakage into the combustion chamber.
	3. Examine the pilot for lack of air (flame will be excessively high).
	4. Check the gas supply and the pilot valve.
	5. Examine the vent assembly filter for clogging.
3. Excessive motor noise	1. If a screeching or howling is present, the air gas mixture is too lean. (See "Pilot Adjustment.")
	2. Check for an imbalance of the blower motor or a motor hum. In either case, the motor must be replaced or serviced.

5 · Electrical System and Refrigeration

The Electrical System

Electrical systems vary according to the age of the camper. The early models contained two separate systems, a 110 volt (V) AC system and a 12 V DC system. Most of the interior components had internal converters that could be switched from 110 V to 12 V when either was available. Light fixtures for this system usually contain two light bulbs per fixture; one for 12 V DC, the other for 110 V AC.

The new system is known as the "uni-volt" system. This has a converter to change 110 V AC current to 12 V DC current by rectifiers and a transformer. Only 12 V appliances can be used in this system. Some units do supply, however, 110 V AC to the wall sockets to power appliances that won't run on 12 V current whenever 110 AC is available.

SYSTEM CONTROL PANEL

Consult your owner's manual to learn the location of the control panel or the fuse box. It's important. It is also good to know which fuse or circuit breaker con-

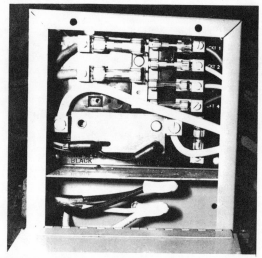

Fuse box (© Airstream Corp.)

trols which camper component. It is a good idea to label the circuit breaker.

Newer trailers use switch type circuit breakers which will trip, moving to the "off" position when overloaded. The switch can be energized once more by moving the switch to the "on" position. Older trailers use the conventional fuse circuit breaker which must be replaced when it is blown.

TRAILER ELECTRICAL CONNECTIONS

Trailer parks will usually supply electricity for a small extra charge. Most modern campers have electrical connections built into the side to accept the three-prong plug common at all parks. This three-prong plug is important since it contains an internal ground wire which is necessary for the camper. Do not use any connections which do not have this wire.

Trailer electrical inlet

WIRING DIAGRAMS

Most of the owners' manuals for the newer campers include a detailed wiring diagram showing the color coding of the wires and the location of the connectors. Keep a copy of this diagram in the trailer at all times because it makes tracing a particular wire much easier.

All the electrical connections in a camper are accessible. There are no connections within the camper walls, but if structural damage is present, the electrical lines running through the skin should be checked.

Electrical Accessories

REFRIGERATOR

There are four types of refrigerating units used in travel trailers: an ice chest; a gas-fired absorption type; an electrically heated absorption type; and an electric compressor type that operates like an air conditioner.

The ice chest type is an insulated compartment built into the cabinets of the kitchen. It is sealed with rubber and the inside surface is lined with plastic. There is insulation between the outer and inner shell. Ice is placed in the unit with the items to be chilled and the sealing around the door helps to keep the inside cold.

The main drawbacks of this system are obvious. Ice, of course, melts and must be replenished. The water has to be drained off often unless there is an automatic drain tube. Also it is impossible to freeze food or keep it frozen in an ice chest.

The gas-operated absorption type of refrigerator is sometimes used in camper trailers. It operates off the propane system that operates the gas lights, stove, oven, and gas hot water heater. This refrigerator is clean, quiet, and very efficient. The system uses gravity, eliminating the need for any compressors, expansion valves, or capillary tubes. Since the system does depend on gravity, the refrigerator must be level. Otherwise the flow of refrigerant will be restricted and the unit will not cool.

In an absorption refrigerator, the refrigerant (ammonia) boils in the evaporator

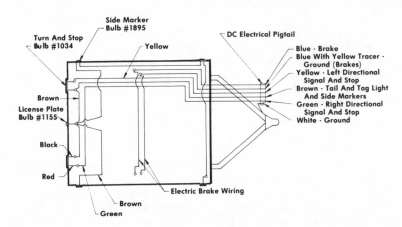

Camper trailer wiring diagram

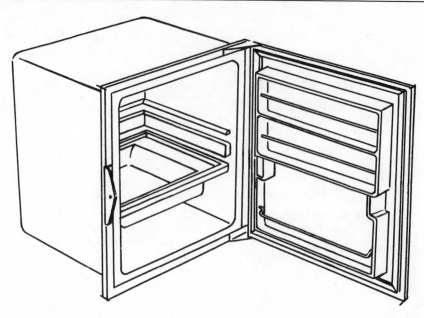

Ice chest type refrigerator

and condenses in the condenser, just as in the mechanical cycle of an air conditioner. Pressure is not the only factor that changes its boiling point, however. During the evaporation process, the ammonia is exposed to hydrogen gas which lowers its boiling point. It evaporates, removing heat from the compartment. The mixture of hydrogen and ammonia gases then drops into an "absorber" chamber containing water which has a strong affinity for the ammonia, but does not attract the hydrogen. This attraction is sufficient for the water to attract all the ammonia in liquid form, condensing it and permitting it to be separated from the hydrogen.

Since hydrogen gas is much lighter than the water-ammonia mixture, it returns to the evaporator. Now the ammonia must be separated from the water if it is to be recovered and reused in the evaporator. The solution of water and ammonia flows into a boiler known as the generator. A gas flame heats the solution in the generator until the tendency of the ammonia to evaporate becomes greater than the water's affinity for it and it is boiled off. Because of the boiling, the ammonia, and some of the water that boils off with it, proceeds through a tube similar to that found in a percolator to a separator known as a rectifier. The heavier liquid, water, is allowed to separate and it drains back to the absorber. On its way, it passes through

its own section of the condenser and is cooled so that it will more readily absorb the ammonia when it gets there. The lighter ammonia gas leaves the rectifier through a pipe leading from the top. It passes through the condenser, where the heat picked up in the generator is removed, and condenses on its way back to the evaporator.

Thus, it is the exposure to hydrogen in the evaporator and the exposure to the water in the absorber that changes the conditions and allows the ammonia to boil and, later, condense. The flame, by heating the ammonia-water solution, provides the energy required to separate the ammonia from the water and to make the refrigerant reusable.

If you have an electric absorption type of refrigerator, the only difference between the one you have and the one described above is that the heating element is electric instead of gas flame. These are more trouble-free than gas-operated refrigerators because of the fewer operating parts but the gas ones are more self-sufficient since they do not require electricity.

The electric compressor type operates in exactly the same way as an air conditioner. The only difference is the absence of a fan or blower to circulate air over the evaporator.

The most frequent trouble with the gas refrigerators is that the pilot light blows

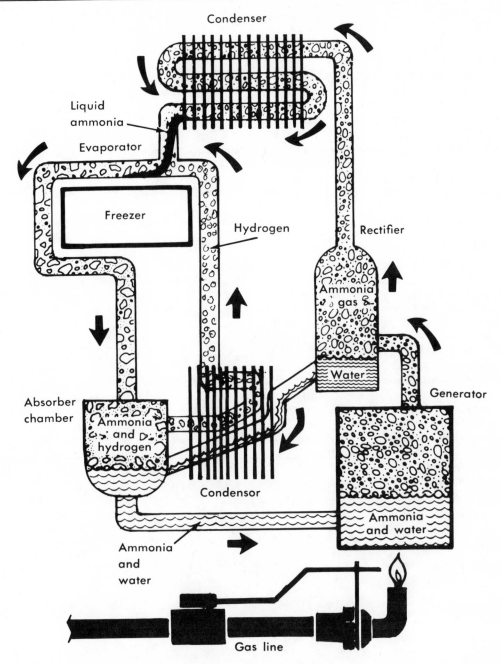

Internal workings of the refrigerator

out. Since the system has a thermocouple, the entire gas supply to the refrigerator is shut off when the pilot goes out. When the pilot light fails to supply enough heat to the thermocouple, it closes a valve by means of a thermo-electrical element which expands and contracts with the application of heat. When this happens, try to light the pilot by pushing down on the button (usually red) and lighting the pilot flame with a match. Keep the button depressed for about a minute, allowing the thermocouple sufficient time to heat and open the gas valve. The pilot should remain lit when the button is released. If it does not, the thermocouple is defective and should be either replaced or repaired. Before replacing the thermocouple, check to see if the heat sensor is right in the middle of the flame. If it is not, adjust it.

The flame should be blue with a yellow tip. If it is all yellow and is giving off soot and an odor, the flame is not burning properly and needs adjustment.

See if you have the right type of burner tip. Some are designed for burning butane and you might be burning propane. Adjust the air flow valves. Check the burner tip for cleanliness. The holes in the tip are particularly small and could very easily become clogged. Do not clean the tip with wire or any metal. It will damage the holes in the tip of the burner jet. Clean the jet in alcohol and blow it dry with compressed air. Lighter fluid is a good substitute for alcohol.

Make sure that the burner points directly at the flue or chimney and in such a way that the proper amount of air can circulate for complete combustion.

The unit should be cleaned yearly. It is a relatively simple job but should not be neglected. Turn the LP gas valve off at the tank and then remove the baffle plate or louver door and remove the flame blow-out guard. Disconnect the gas pipeline from the pipe nipple, being careful not to damage the nut. Remove the pipe nipple which holds the jet as a unit in alcohol or lighter fluid. Blow it dry with compressed air. Remember that no metal object is to be inserted into the holes of the jet. Clean the burner tube (generator), paying close attention to the gauze. Use a brush or a cloth and blow it out with air. It is not necessary to remove the burner tube for cleaning; just make sure that you cover the burner jet with a clean cloth so that debris from the burner tube does not fall down on the jet. When you replace the parts that have been serviced, be sure to check for leaks. Use the soapy water solution on all of the joints and check for bubbles.

Many trailer owners want their refrigerators to operate while they drive. This is not recommended, but, in theory, most units should operate when towing. The motion of the trailer is much the same as a ship that is rolling in high seas. It passes from side to side and is out of level "equally" in all directions. It must also pass through the level stage every so often, circulating the refrigeration gases and liquids, even though at a restricted rate. The only problem that could possibly arise, and usually does, is that of keeping the pilot lit.

If the refrigeration system needs to be repaired, take the unit to a qualified refrigeration mechanic. Refrigerant is corrosive and hydrogen is explosive and the whole system is under high pressure. If the sealed system goes bad, the entire unit will probably have to be replaced anyway, so there is really nothing that can be done in the way of repairs.

Refrigerator Troubleshooting Chart

Condition	Remedy
The pilot will not light.	Check the LP tank to see if it is empty. Look for damaged or blocked gas line.
The pilot goes out when the button is released.	Check the thermocouple; it is most likely defective. Make sure that the heat sensor is properly positioned in the flame.
The pilot lights but the flame is low.	The LP gas tank is nearly empty. The refrigerator thermostat is defective and has to be replaced. The burner jets are dirty or clogged and need to be cleaned.
The refrigerator does not cool satisfactorily.	There is a restricted vent. Remove any restriction. The refrigerator is not level. The gas bottle is used up. The thermocouple is not being heated enough by the flame. Adjust it or replace it. The burner jet or the burner gauze is clogged. Clean the jet as described in the text and clean the gauze with a brush. If your unit is designed to have a flue baffle in the exhaust flue, the problem might lie there. The baffle is designed to distribute heat and cause proper air flow. It may be missing altogether or be installed at the wrong height inside the flue. The gas pressure at the burner is incorrect. The burner assembly may not be secured properly and is moving around when the trailer is being towed. The thermostat may be at the wrong setting. Turn it to a higher number. The refrigerating unit has failed. The gases in the unit may have become separated and formed a "vapor lock." If possible, take the unit out of the cabinet and turn it upside down several times so that the liquid in the boiler can be mixed with the liquid in the absorber vessel. This procedure will restore the liquid balance in the unit.
The refrigerator is too cold.	The thermostat is set at the wrong setting. Turn the dial to a lower number. Dirt in the valve of the thermostat. Clean the valve and the valve seat in the thermostat.

6 · Chassis Maintenance

Running Gear Assembly

Most camper trailers have an underslung spring arrangement. The spring ends point upward and are attached to the chassis while the axle assembly is attached to the underside or top of the spring by U-bolts and a flat plate. This arrangement is common for both single-axle and double-axle trailers.

Another popular design is the torsional spring suspension. This consists of a square torsion bar mounted inside a metal casing with rubber cords, known as elastomers, on each of the four sides of the torsion bar and the inside of the casing. When the bar twists in the casing, it compresses the rubber cords which allow the torsion bar to turn only a limited distance. The trailer is, in effect, mounted on rubber springs. There is no contact of any metal parts between the wheel and the chassis so

Leaf spring assembly

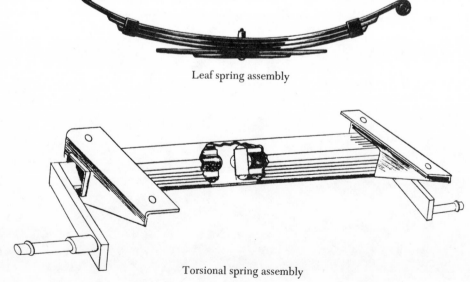

Torsional spring assembly

this system provides a smoother and quieter spring action. Since each wheel acts independently of the other, trailer sway is diminished considerably. This type of suspension was first used on lighter trailers such as boat trailers. It has since been perfected and adapted to use on heavier trailers.

AXLE REMOVAL

Underslung Spring Suspension

1. Jack up the trailer so all the wheels are raised off the ground at least 1 in. Put jackstands under the tongue at the front end and at a suitable location at the rear of the trailer. It is very important to consult each individual owner's manual for the proper jacking instructions and locations.
2. Remove the wheel and tire assembly.
3. Disconnect all electric brake wires and hydraulic brake lines.
4. Remove the upper attachments of the shock absorbers and any axle locating arms.
5. Support the axle at the center with a floor jack.
6. Remove the nuts and washers from the U-bolts at both ends of the axle.
7. Lower the axle with the floor jack or slide the axle off the spring on one side, then down and out from beneath the trailer.
8. Check the axle for cracks and other damage. Check the shock absorbers for leakage and other damage.
9. To replace, reverse the above procedure.

Torsional Spring Suspension

The procedure for removing the axle from trailers with torsional spring suspensions is exactly the same as for underslung types except for step 6. Instead of removing nuts and washers from the U-bolts holding the axle up to the springs, the nuts, bolts, and washers holding the axle mounting plate to the chassis of the trailer will be removed.

NOTE: *It is not recommended that the tongue jack be used alone for supporting the front end of the trailer. Jackstands should be placed under each front side of the trailer. Also after removal and replacement of the axles from trailers with hydraulic brakes, be sure to bleed the brakes at the wheel cylinder. See the brake section for bleeding procedures.*

AXLE ALIGNMENT

The most convenient method of checking to see if the wheels or axles are properly aligned is to check the tire for irregular wear patterns. To understand axle alignment, it is, therefore, necessary to understand tire wear patterns.

Underinflation is probably the greatest cause of excessive tire wear. When the tire is underinflated, it will only wear on the outer edges. This is due to the high profile of the trailer which will rock from side to side on soft tires. The tires on the curb side will usually wear faster than the tires on the road side since road surfaces usually slant down from the center out. This causes the trailer to lean toward the curb and forces the outer edge of the tire to roll under.

Improper toe-in is the second most common cause of abnormal tire wear. A tire that has too much toe-in or toe-out will side-slip on the road surface as it is traveling along. This type of misalignment will cause the tread of the tire to wear with a sharp edge on one side and a round edge on the other. A tire with an excessive amount of toe-out will wear the inside edge of the tire and the sharp edge of the tread will be pointing toward the outside. A tire with too much toe-in will wear the outside of the tread, much the same way that an underinflated tire would do, but the grooves of the tread will have the sharp edges on the inside of the tread surface.

Camber is probably the least cause of alignment problems. The camber adjustment has to be extremely out of tolerance before any noticeable wear is observed. A tire or wheel with too much positive camber will wear the outer half of the tire and a tire with too much negative camber will wear the inner half of the tire. In both cases, the tread will wear evenly around the tire, not in spots as with improper toe-in.

Since alignment of the axles calls for special tools, equipment, and knowledge, it is no job for the back yard mechanic.

Most alignment is done by bending the axle horizontally or vertically—depending on which adjustment is being made. Bending forward or backward adjusts toe-in and toe-out; up or down adjusts camber. Very powerful hydraulic benders are clamped to the axle and pressure is applied gradually—to prevent damaging it —to bend the axle to the manufacturer's specifications. Never heat the axle because heat destroys the temper. Also, heat will destroy the rubber elastomers of torsional spring axles.

WHEEL AND TIRE MAINTENANCE

Pressure is the most important part of tire maintenance. If proper pressure is maintained, maximum tire life can be expected. Since tire pressure gauges are inexpensive, it's a good idea to get one and keep it in the trailer. Use it often, but only when the tires are cool. Pressure increases at running temperatures and a hot tire would give a deceptive reading. Be careful not to bleed the tires when they are hot.

Tires should be rotated after 5,000 miles. Consult your owner's manual for the proper rotating pattern.

Proper wheel balance is important because the extreme vibration of an imbalanced wheel could eventually cause structural damage to the trailer. The wheel should be balanced every time the tires are rotated or repaired.

When changing a tire, consult the owner's manual for proper jacking instructions and locations.

After the wheel assembly is replaced on the hub, tighten the lug nuts diametrically to the recommended torque. If a torque wrench is not available, tighten the lug nuts with a regular lug wrench to a reasonable tightness, being careful not to stretch the wheel stud or break it off.

WHEEL BEARINGS

Wheel bearing maintenance for trailers is something that can be handled by anyone with a bit of automotive knowledge, sufficient and suitable wheel bearing grease, and a few basic tools such as a screwdriver and a pair of pliers.

Before handling the bearings, however,

Troubleshooting Wheel/Tire Assembly

Wheel Shimmy

Probable Cause	Remedy
Loose wheel lug nuts	Tighten to 110 ft lbs
Loose or broken wheel bearing	Tighten spindle nut or replace and adjust wheel bearing
Wheel out of balance	Balance the wheel
Bent wheel	Replace the wheel
Improper axle alignment	Have axle aligned to manufacturer's specifications

Improper Tire Wear

Probable Cause	Remedy
Not rotating the tires	Rotate tires according to manufacturer's recommendations in owner's manual, or by an authorized mechanic at a trailer service center
Incorrect air pressure	Inflate the tires to proper pressure
Improperly acting brake	Correct as required
Improper axle alignment	Align axle

Bearing cross section

there are a few things that you should try to remember and a few to avoid.

Remember to:

1. Remove all outside dirt from the housing before exposing the bearing;

2. Treat a used bearing as gently as you would a new one;

3. Work with clean tools, in a clean area;

4. Use clean, dry canvas gloves, or at least clean, dry hands;

5. Use clean solvents and flushing fluids;

6. Lay the bearings on clean paper to dry;

7. Protect disassembled bearings from rust and dirt by covering them;

8. Use clean rags to wipe bearings;

9. Keep the bearings in oil-proof paper when they are to be stored or are not in use;

10. Clean the inside of the housing before replacing the bearing.

Avoid:

1. Working in dirty surroundings;

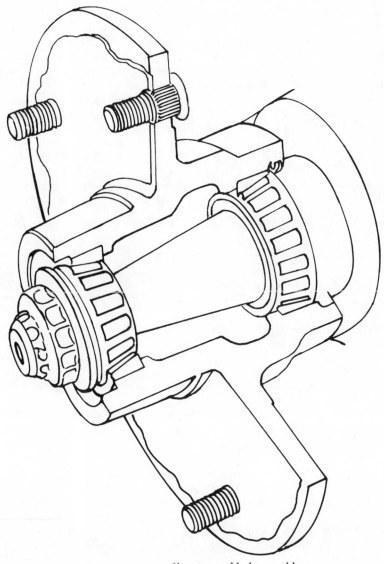

Cutaway view of bearing and hub assembly

2. Using dirty, chipped, or damaged tools;

3. Working on wooden benches or using wooden mallets;

4. Handling bearings with dirty or moist hands;

5. Using gasoline; use a safe solvent instead;

6. Spin drying bearings with compressed air. They will spin at a far greater speed than they are designed to withstand;

7. Spinning unclean bearings;

8. Using cotton waste or dirty cloths to wipe bearings;

9. Scratching or nicking bearing surfaces;

10. Allowing the bearing to come in contact with dirt or rust at any time.

The procedure for checking and/or replacing wheel bearings is as follows.

1. Jack up the trailer so the wheels are off the ground and can spin freely. Consult the owner's manual for proper jacking instructions and locations. Since it is easier to check all the bearings at the same time, raise the trailer off all its wheels by using jackstands or blocks, if possible. Make sure the trailer is completely stable before continuing.

2. Remove the hub cap and the dust cap with a heavy screwdriver. Some dust caps screw on; a pair of water pump pliers will be needed to remove these.

3. Remove the cotter pin and discard it. Cotter pins should never be reused.

4. Remove the spindle nut and the washer behind it.

5. Wiggle the hub and wheel assembly so the outer wheel bearing becomes loose and can be removed.

6. Remove the wheel and hub assembly from the spindle and place it on the ground with the outside facing up.

7. Place a block of wood down through the spindle hole and tap out the inner grease seal. Never use anything made of metal to tap out the grease seal because the inner bearing can be damaged. Tap lightly. When the seal falls out, so will the inner bearing. Discard the seal. Perform the above procedures to all the wheels that are to be serviced.

NOTE: *Some small camper trailers do not use inner bearings or seals.*

8. Place all of the bearings, nuts, washers, and dust caps in a container of solvent and clean each part thoroughly with a light soft brush or an oil paint brush. Make sure that every bit of dirt and grease is rinsed off, then place each cleaned part on an absorbent cloth and let them dry completely.

9. Inspect the bearings for pitting, flat spots, rust, and rough areas. Check the races on the hub and the spindle for the same defects. Rub them clean with a rag soaked in solvent. If they show hairline cracks or worn, shiny areas, they must be replaced with new parts. Replacement seals, bearings, and other required parts can be bought at any auto parts store or trailer service center. The old parts that are to be replaced should be taken along to be compared with the replacement part to ensure a perfect match.

10. Pack the wheel bearings with grease. There are special tools to grease wheel bearings but don't buy one if you don't have it. Wheel bearings can be packed by hand by putting a large dab of grease in the palm of your hand and pushing the bearing through it with a sliding motion. The grease must be forced through the side of the bearing and in between each roller. Keep this up until the grease begins to ooze out the other side and through the gaps between the rollers. The bearing must be completely packed with grease.

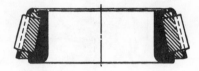

Trailer bearing with the shaded ares representing the positioning of the grease

There is a special wheel bearing grease for trailers; it has longer fibers than the type used on cars. The reason for this is that when trailer axles are made, the spindle is machined before the axle is bent to the desired shape. The spindle is sometimes bent slightly out of round in the process. Trailer bearings are, therefore, slightly more susceptible to failure than those on a car. To compensate for this unfortunate condition, special grease with longer fibers (to take up the gap that is created between the bearing and the imperfect surface of the spindle) is used. Be sure to use the special trailer bearing grease which can be obtained from any well-equipped trailer service center.

11. Turn the hub assembly over, making sure that it is perfectly clean, and drop the inner wheel bearing into place. Using a hammer and a block of wood, tap the new seal in place. Do not hit the race with the hammer directly. Move the block of wood around the circumference until it is seated properly.

Installing the inner wheel bearing and seal

NOTE: *On small campers, only the outer bearing is inserted; there are no inner bearings.*

12. Slide the hub and wheel assembly onto the spindle and push it as far as it will go, making sure that it has completely covered the brake shoes.

Installing the hub and the drum

13. Place the outer bearing over the spindle and press it in until it is snug. Place the drum on the spindle behind the bearing. Next, put the spindle nut on and turn it down until a slight binding is felt, then back it off to the nearest notch and place the new cotter pin through the notch

Positioning the outside bearings

and the hole in the spindle. Bend one end of the cotter pin up and over the end of the spindle and cut off the other end with a pair of cutters.

Locknut adjustment and the insertion of the cotter pin

14. Replace the dust cap and the hub cap. The dust cap must fit snugly to protect the bearings from dust, water, and the like. If it looks as though it might not be able to seal the hub properly, replace it.

Bearing Diagnosis

This section will help in the diagnosis of bearing failure and the causes. Bearing diagnosis can be very helpful in determining the causes of rear axle failure. The illustrations will help to take some of the guesswork out of determining when to reuse a bearing and when to replace a bearing with a new one.

When disassembling a rear axle, the general condition of all bearings should be noted and classified where possible. Proper recognition of the cause will help in correcting the problem and avoiding a repetition of the failure. Some of the common causes of bearing failure are:

1. Abuse during assembly or disassembly;
2. Improper assembly methods;
3. Improper or inadequate lubrication;
4. Bearing contact with dirt or water;
5. Wear caused by dirt or metal chips;
6. Corrosion or rust;
7. Seizing due to overloading;
8. Overheating;
9. Frettage of the bearing seats;
10. Brinelling from impact or shock loading;
11. Manufacturing defects;
12. Pitting due to fatigue.

To avoid damage to the bearing from improper handling, treat a used bearing the same as a new bearing. Always work in a clean area with clean tools. Remove all outside dirt from the housing before exposing a bearing and clean all bearing seats before installing a bearing.

CAUTION: *Never spin a bearing, either by hand or with compressed air, as this will lead to almost certain bearing failure.*

Bearing Failure Chart

General Wear

Cause	Serviceability
Wear on races and rollers caused by fine abrasives.	Clean all parts and check seals. Install new bearing if old one is rough or noisy.

General wear (© Chevolet Div. G.M. Corp.)

Step Wear

Cause	Serviceability
Wear pattern on roller ends caused by fine abrasives.	Clean all parts and check seals. Install new bearing if old one is rough or noisy.

Step wear (© Chevolet Div. G.M. Corp.)

Indentations

Cause	Serviceability
Surface depressions on races and rollers caused by hard foreign particles.	Clean all parts and check seals. Install new bearing if old one is rough or noisy.

Indentations (© Chevrolet Div. G.M. Corp.)

Galling

Cause	Serviceability
Metal smears on roller ends due to overheating from improper lubricant or overloading.	Install a new bearing. Check seals and be sure proper lubricant is used.

Galling (© Chevrolet Div. G.M. Corp.)

Bearing Failure Chart

Etching

Cause	Serviceability
Bearing surfaces appear gray or grayish black with related etching.	Install new bearing and check seals. Be sure proper lubricant is used.

Etching (© Chevrolet Div. G.M. Corp.)

Cage Wear

Cause	Serviceability
Wear around outside diameter of cage and rollers caused by foreign material and poor lubrication.	Clean all parts, check the seals and install new bearing.

Cage wear (© Chevrolet Div. G.M. Corp.)

Fatigue Spalling

Cause	Serviceability
Flaking of surface metal due to fatigue.	Clean all parts and install new bearing.

Fatigue spalling (© Chevrolet Div. G.M. Corp.)

Stain Discoloration

Cause	Serviceability
Stain discoloration ranging from light brown to black, caused by lubricant breakdown or moisture.	Re-use bearings if stains can be removed by light polishing and no overheating exists. Check seals for damage.

Stain discoloration (© Chevrolet Div. G.M. Corp.)

Heat Discoloration

Cause	Serviceability
Discoloration can range from faint yellow to dark blue due to overload or lubricant breakdown. Softening of races or rollers can also occur.	Check for softening of parts by drawing a file over suspected area. The file will glide easily over hard metal, but will cut soft metal. If overheating is evident, install new bearings. Check seals and other parts.

Heat discoloration (© Chevrolet Div. G.M. Corp.)

Bearing Failure Chart

Brinelling

Cause	Serviceability
Surface indentations in the race caused by rollers under impact load or vibration while the bearing is not rotating.	If the old bearing is rough or noisy, install a new bearing.

Brinelling (© Chevrolet Div. G.M. Corp.)

Bent Cage

Cause	Serviceability
Due to improper handling.	Install a new bearing.

Bent cage (© Chevrolet Div. G.M. Corp.)

Bent Cage

Cause	Serviceability
Due to improper handling.	Install a new bearing.

Bent cage (© Chevrolet Div. G.M. Corp.)

Misalignment

Cause	Serviceability
Outer race misaligned as shown.	Install a new bearing and be sure races and bearing are properly seated.

Misalignment (© Chevrolet Div. G.M. Corp.)

Cracked Inner Race

Cause	Serviceability
Crack due to improper fit, cocked bearing or poor bearing seats.	Install a new bearing and be sure it is seated properly.

Cracked inner race (© Chevrolet Div. G.M. Corp.)

Bearing Failure Chart

Frettage

Cause	Serviceability
Corrosion due to small movement of parts with no lubrication.	Clean parts and check seals. Install a new bearing and be sure of proper lubrication.

Frettage (© Chevrolet Div. G.M. Corp.)

Smears

Cause	Serviceability
Metal smears due to slippage caused by poor fit, improper lubrication, overloading or handling damage.	Clean parts, install new bearing and check for proper fit and proper lubrication.

Smears (© Chevrolet Div. G.M. Corp.)

Electric Brakes

Electric brakes are operated by 12 V current from the tow vehicle and are integrally connected with the tow vehicle's brake system. The controller, which is hooked up to the tow vehicle's master cylinder and battery, transfers surge pressure from the master cylinder into electrical current. The controller can be set to determine when the trailer brakes start to operate in relation to the amount of pressure exerted on the car's brake pedal. A variable resistor regulates the amount of current coming from the controller and going to the brake assemblies. It can be adjusted according to how much electrical power is needed at the brakes, based on the total trailer weight.

When the brake pedal is applied, surge pressure is received from the tow vehicle's master cylinder by the controller's hydraulic cylinder. The controller's hydraulic cylinder pushes down on a set of points which completes a circuit from the tow vehicle's battery to the variable resistor. The electric current flows through the resistor and is decreased to the desired amount, according to how the variable resistor is set up. The proper amount of current then flows through the electrical coupling between the tow vehicle and the trailer and then on to the brakes. The electric current activates the magnet assembly causing it to attach itself to a steel armature plate that rotates with the brake drum. The magnet tries to rotate with the armature plate and, in fact, does move slightly, causing the arm to which the magnet is secured to move and expand the brake shoes against the brake drums.

There are various types of controllers available. The three basic designs all operate in a similar manner. The completely automatic model (in that the driver does not have to handle the controller in any way to operate it) is usually mounted under the dash or under the hood. This type is hooked into the tow vehicle's hydraulic braking system and is activated automatically when the brake pedal is, pushed. The only disadvantage to this type of system is that the trailer brakes cannot be applied separately without the tow vehicle's brakes also being applied. The manually operated controller (in that the driver has to operate the controller by hand every time the trailer brakes are needed) is usually mounted either on the steering column or dash where the controlling lever is convenient to the driver. When the driver wishes to stop using both car and trailer brakes, the brake pedal and the controller lever must be applied simultaneously. This is obviously inconvenient since you must reach down for the controlling lever every time the brake pedal is depressed.

The third type of controller can be operated manually or can be left to operate automatically. It is integrally connected with the tow vehicle's brake system and is activated by pushing the brake pedal. It also

Electric brake wheel assembly

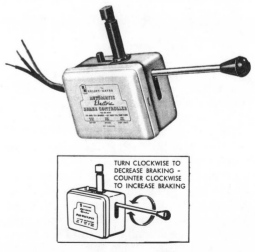

Steering column controller assembly

has a controller lever which lets it be operated manually, allowing the driver to apply the trailer brakes separately if so desired. This controller is also mounted on the steering column or dash to give the driver access to the controller lever.

The handle protruding from the control unit serves two purposes: it determines (by point gap setting) when to initiate the flow of electric current from the tow vehicle's battery and on to the rest of the system. The lever also serves as the variable resistor adjustment. The variable resistor is usually incorporated into the control box of those controllers with levers. The system activation is accomplished by depressing the handle. The variable resistor setting is made by rotating the handle in either direction, thus increasing or decreasing the amount of current needed at the brakes.

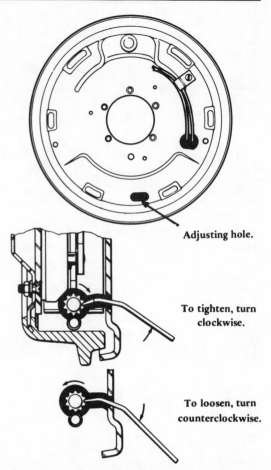

Adjusting hole.

To tighten, turn clockwise.

To loosen, turn counterclockwise.

Adjusting hole location and brake adjusting method (© Airstream Corp.)

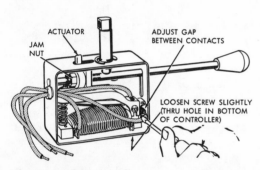

Adjustment of the controller

BRAKE ADJUSTMENT

1. Electric brakes should be adjusted every 5,000 miles or every year, whichever comes first.

2. Block the wheels so the trailer won't move.

3. Jack the trailer so the wheels just clear the ground.

NOTE: *It is extremely important to consult each individual owner's manual for proper jacking instructions. Failure to do so could result in serious damage to the trailer.*

4. Remove the small rubber plug at the base of the backing plate.

5. While spinning the wheel, tighten the brakes by turning the star adjuster wheel. A brake adjusting tool or a screwdriver bent to a 90° angle will do the job properly. Turn the star adjuster until the wheel has a heavy drag, then back up the adjuster about 10 or 12 notches until the wheel

turns freely. There must be no drag present after the adjusting procedure is completed. Electric brakes must "hit" the drum fairly hard to be effective on trailers. To accomplish this they must travel farther, so the adjustment must be backed off more than would be common practice on an automobile.

6. Replace the rubber plug.

7. Repeat the above procedure for all trailer wheels.

BRAKE ASSEMBLY AND INSTALLATION

1. Block the wheels so the trailer won't move.

2. Jack the trailer so the wheel is off the ground. Once again, consult the owner's manual for proper jacking instructions.

3. Remove the hub cap and dust cap.

4. Remove the cotter pin.

5. Remove the spindle nut and washer.

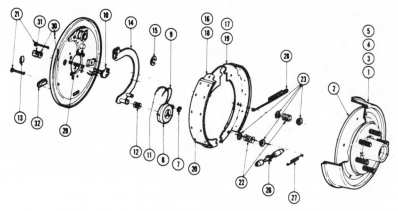

Exploded view of the brake assembly (© Airstream Corp.)

1. Brake assembly	11. Terminal insulation (red)	21. Hold down pin
2. Armature plate	12. Magnet spring	22. Hold down spring
3. Washer	13. Cable clip	23. Hold down cup
4. Nut	14. Lever	26. Adjusting screw assy.
5. Screw	15. Lever retaining rings	27. Adjusting screw spring
6. Screw	16. Shoe & lining assy. pri.	28. Retractor spring
7. Magnet assembly	17. Shoe & lining assy. sec.	29. Brake mounting stud
8. Retaining ring	18. Lining primary	30. Brake mounting washer
9. Terminal (12-V green)	19. Lining secondary	31. Brake mounting nut
10. Terminal butt connector	20. Rivets	32. Brake adj. hole cover

6. Remove the outer bearing.

7. Remove the wheel, hub, brake drum, and inner bearing all in one assembly.

8. Remove the brake shoes by removing all springs, retainers, and hold-down pins. Take note of their location so they can be replaced in the same position. Special brake tools are available to facilitate the removal and installation of brake shoes. If none are available, a screwdriver and a pair of pliers can be used. Caution should be exercised when removing or installing springs because of the high spring tension.

9. Remove the star adjustment wheel from the bottom of the brake shoes. Make sure that the star wheel turns freely. A drop of light lubricating oil on the threads is recommended. When the star wheel is replaced on the new brake shoes, it should be adjusted to about the halfway point.

10. Apply a small amount of Lubriplate® to the backing plate where the shoes rub.

11. To install, reverse the above procedure. Be sure the bearings and races are clean before installing. Tighten the spindle nut until it is snug then back off one notch and install a new cotter pin. Adjust the brakes. (See Brake Adjustment.)

Inspect the armature plates. Under nor-

Armature Surface

Brake drum armature surface

mal conditions they should last indefinitely. If the plate shows excessive wear, though (due to sand, mud, small stones), replace it. If only one armature plate is bad, it is not necesssary to replace them all. If the armature plate is riveted in place, the rivets can be drilled out; the replacement part can be installed with screws, nuts, and lockwashers.

NOTE: *Always inspect the magnet assembly when replacing the armature plate since the same condition that damaged it could also damage the magnet. If the magnet is wearing flat, there is no need to replace it unless it shows signs of wearing through to the magnet coil. (See "Checking the Magnet Assembly.")*

Checking the surface of the magnet assembly for level

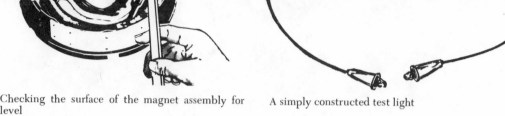

A simply constructed test light

Brake Drums

Inspect the brake drum rubbing surface. It should have a dull gray appearance but one or two light score marks are no cause for alarm. If heavy scoring and excessive wear are present, however, the rubbing surface should be rebored or cut. Be sure that no more than the recommended amount is taken off the rubbing surface and that the inside diameter of the drum is not extended beyond the recommended limits.

NOTE: *After cutting or reboring a brake drum, the brake lining may have to be ground to coincide with the new diameter of the drum. Some linings may even require shims between the lining and the shoe. Also adjust the brakes after having the drum cut or rebored.*

Brake Lining

Inspect the lining for wear. If worn to the rivets or past the minimum thickness, replace it. Look for uneven wear patterns which will indicate improperly located flanges or a bent backing plate. If the lining is badly contaminated with grease or oil, replace it; this type of damage cannot be sanded or dissolved out of the brake lining.

NOTE: *Always replace brake linings in sets, both shoes on the same axle.*

ELECTRICAL COMPONENT CHECK

When making any electrical tests, hook up the trailer to the tow vehicle.

Check continuity with a test light at three locations; inside the tow vehicle, between the control box and the trailer power lead to the car-trailer electrical plug; at the trailer tongue between the breakaway switch and the power lead; and at the brake assembly at each wheel.

Checking the Controller

Hook into the trailer power lead at the controller but operate the controller slowly. The test light should begin to glow and increase in brightness at a steady rate as the handle or brake pedal is depressed. If the test light operates, and increases and decreases smoothly in intensity, the controller is operating correctly. If the test light does not perform as above, the controller should be checked for the following problems:

Circuit Check

1. Check the connector plug for proper contact and cleanliness.
2. Check all terminal points and splices in the tow vehicle and the trailer for proper contacts and bare wires that might be shorting out the system.
3. Check for a blown fuse in the tow vehicle portion of the circuit.

Controller Check

Connect one lead of the test light to the trailer power lead and ground the other lead to the vehicle. Operate the controller. The current should vary smoothly and the test light should gradually get brighter as the controller lever is depressed. If the light does not brighten smoothly or there is no current present at all, remove the controller cover and inspect the resistor coil. If the coil, which should last indefinitely, is burned out, something is drastically wrong. (This can be detected visually.) The entire electrical system should be checked for a short circuit which could destroy any electric brake controller.

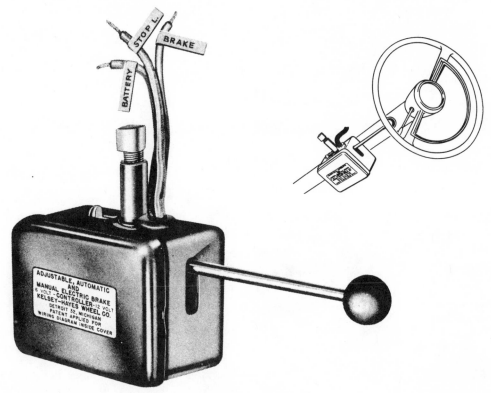

Controller assembly

Be sure to set the prescribed gap clearance between the contactor strip and the resistor coil after replacing the coil. The gap can usually be adjusted by loosening one screw through an access hole in the bottom of the controller case. This setting is what determines when the electric brakes start to work after the pedal is pushed. The wider the setting, the farther the brake pedal has to be pushed before the brakes go down.

Inspect the hydraulic cylinder inside, and its fittings outside, for leakage while checking the controller. If leakage is present from the cylinder, it should be replaced. If leakage is originating at one of the fittings, try to tighten the fitting, but if this does not help, the fitting should be replaced. After replacement of the hydraulic cylinder in the controller, the line is to be bled at the controller.

Checking the Breakaway Switch

The breakaway switch is located on the tongue and serves as an emergency braking system for the trailer if it accidentally uncouples from the tow vehicle. The switch is usually connected to the tow vehicle by a small chain or cable. If the trailer separates from the car, the cable pulls out a pin or activates the switch. The switch then draws current from its own power source, usually two or three dry cell batteries or the trailer's self-contained power source, and activates the trailer brakes.

The breakaway switch can be checked by placing a test light in the circuit between the switch and the brakes and then activating the switch by pulling out the pin. If no current flows to the brakes, check the breakaway switch contacts for cleanliness and proper contact.

Another way of checking the switch is by jacking up the trailer and having someone spin a wheel while the switch is activated. If the switch is operating correctly the brakes should lock the wheel.

Check the batteries or trailer battery for adequate charge and replace them as necessary.

Checking the Magnet Assembly

Inspect the magnet for wear and flatness. If the rubbing surface doesn't show

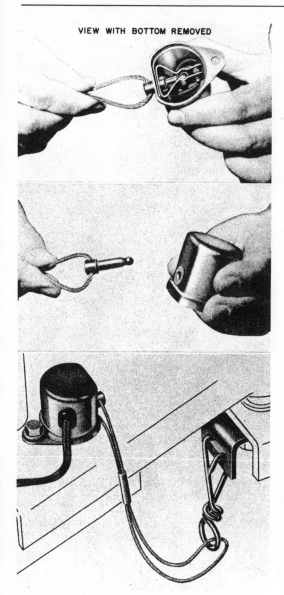

Operation of a breakaway switch

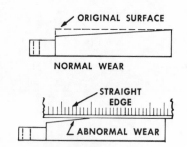

Checking the magnet assembly

mature plate unevenly. In this case, the lever assembly should be replaced. When installing magnets be careful not to crimp or squash the wires and to allow ample clearance for movement of the lever and the other moving parts.

To check for an electrical short in the magnet assembly, remove the magnet from the brake assembly and connect a test light in a series with the magnet assembly and the tow vehicle's 12 V battery. Since the short may occur intermittently, move the lead ends and rap the magnet while checking it. If the light does not react or flickers, the magnet is defective and should be replaced.

The Variable Resistor

As explained in the beginning paragraphs of this section, the variable resistor regulates the maximum braking capacity of the trailer brakes. Because of the wide range in axle loading, the rated maximum load braking capacity of the brakes may exceed the actual braking needs of a particular trailer. Thus the need for a selective resistor. The resistor has various settings according to the maximum trailer weight. Some resistors have setting diagrams to follow but if no diagram is present, a qualified trailer mechanic should make the correct setting on the resistor. After the resistor is installed on the tow vehicle and set according to the proper specifications, check the application of the trailer brakes with the controller fully ap-

signs of rubbing through and is wearing in the proper manner, don't replace it. To check the magnet for the proper wear pattern, lay a scale or straightedge on the rubbing surface; it should be flat all the way across. If the magnet is not wearing properly, it must be replaced. It cannot work at top efficiency if the entire rubbing surface is not making contact with the armature plate.

Before replacing the defective magnet, determine the cause of the improper wear. Check the magnet lever pivot. A worn pivot can cause the magnet lever to cock, allowing the magnet to rest upon the ar-

Variable resistor

plied. With the controller fully on, the brakes should provide firm braking action just short of the tires skidding on dry pavement.

Surge Brakes

Surge brakes are similar to car brakes in that they are operated by hydraulic pressure. There is a master cylinder that compresses brake fluid in the lines, which in turn expands wheel cylinders at the brakes and presses the brake shoes against the drums. The only difference between surge brakes and electric brakes is the way in which they are activated. Though electric brakes seem to be more popular presently, this does not mean that hydraulic brakes are not as effective. In fact it is said that hydraulic brakes operate more smoothly than electric ones.

Surge brake hitch assembly

The master cylinder that operates those trailer brakes with a surge system is located on the tongue of the trailer. When the tow vehicle slows down, the momentum of the trailer pushes or "surges" against the hitch ball and activates the master cylinder. Pressure is then sent

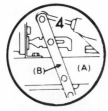

Trailer tongue A moves forward with the stopping of the car and moves linkage B which activates the plunger in the master cylinder.

through the brake lines to the wheel cylinders which press the brake shoes against the drums.

The breakaway switch on surge brakes operates in a similar manner to those on electric brakes. The purpose is the same—to provide emergency braking for the trailer in case of an accidental separation of the tow vehicle and the trailer. The breakaway switch is connected to the tow vehicle by a chain or a cable when the trailer is under tow. If the trailer becomes disconnected, the cable pulls on a lever which is connected to a tooth bar so it cannot return without being released by hand. The lever pushes in on the master cylinder, activating the brakes.

MAINTENANCE

The maintenance procedures for hydraulic brakes are similar to those for electric brakes in many ways. The procedures for removing the brake shoes and installing them, checking for proper wear patterns on the brake shoes and drums, and having the drums cut are all the same.

The Master Cylinder

The master cylinder is to be inspected frequently for leakage and to make sure the proper level of brake fluid is maintained in the reservoir. If the cylinder shows signs of leaking, replace it. If the fluid level in the reservoir is below the prescribed level and continues to drip after being refilled, there is a leak somewhere. To check for a leak, inspect all connections in the brake lines. To check the wheel cylinders, remove the wheel as-

Hydraulic brake assembly

sembly and the brake drum. Refer to the section on electric brakes to remove the wheel assembly and drum. Once the wheel cylinder is exposed, look for surfaces coated with brake fluid and replace them. If there is no immediate evidence of leakage, pull back the dust covers on the wheel cylinder itself. If fluid is present just inside the dust cover, the wheel cylinder is leaking. Rebuild or replace it.

Rebuilding the Wheel Cylinders

1. Assuming that the trailer has been jacked up properly, the wheels have been blocked (refer to the electric brake section and also the owner's manual), and the wheel assembly and drum have been removed, remove the brake shoes.

2. Remove the dust covers or boots from the cylinder ends and discard them. Remove the pistons, remove and discard the seal cups, and remove the expanders and spring.

3. Inspect the bore and pistons for damage or wear. Damaged pistons should be discarded as they cannot be reconditioned. Slight bore roughness can be removed by using a brake cylinder hone or crocus cloth with a fine grain. The cloth should be rotated in the bore under finger pressure. Do not slide the cloth lengthwise.

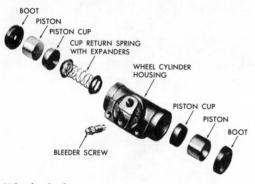

BOOT
PISTON
PISTON CUP
CUP RETURN SPRING
WITH EXPANDERS
WHEEL CYLINDER
HOUSING
PISTON CUP
PISTON
BOOT
BLEEDER SCREW

Wheel cylinder components

4. Clean the cylinder and internal parts with brake fluid.

5. Insert the spring expander assembly. Lubricate all rubber parts with fresh brake fluid.

6. Install new cups with the seal lips facing inward.

7. Install the pistons and rubber boots.

8. Replace the brake shoes and the wheel, drum assembly.

9. Bleed the system at the wheel cylinder.

Bleeding the Brakes

1. Fill the reservoir of the master cylinder with brake fluid.

2. While pressure is being applied to the master cylinder by pushing the breakaway switch lever against the master cylinder, loosen the bleed screw on the wheel cylinder about a quarter of a turn. This will allow air in the line and wheel cylinder to escape.

3. Refill the master cylinder with brake fluid and repeat the above procedure until no air—just brake fluid—comes out of the bleed screw.

4. Fill the master cylinder with brake fluid.

NOTE: *If the wheel cylinder is completely replaced the system still must be bled at the wheel cylinder.*

Brake Adjustment

The brake adjustment procedure for hydraulic brakes is very similar to that for electric brakes. The only difference is that, when the star adjuster wheel is backed off, there should still be slight drag of the brakes when the wheel is spun by hand. Make sure that each wheel is adjusted so that there is approximately the same amount of drag on each wheel. (Refer to the electric brake section for the exact brake adjusting procedures.)

Brake Troubleshooting Chart

Problem: Locking or Grabbing Brakes

Probable Cause	Solution
Controller not modulating	Check wiring for worn covering, broken wires, and wires that may be shorting out the system. Check with a test light.
Grease or brake fluid on the lining	Replace the seals or dust caps and replace the brake lining.
Wrong brake lining	Change the linings to all the same brand and material.
Rust in the armature plate and/or the brake drums	Drum and armature may rust from non-use; condition is usually corrected by continued normal use.
Loose parts	Remove the hub and look for broken springs or loose rivets jammed in the brakes.
Excessive braking power	Install a selective resistor or adjust the selective resistor.

Problem: Weak Brakes

Probable Cause	Solution
Improper adjustment	Adjust the brakes to compensate for wear.
Poor connections	Check to be sure that all connections are clean and tight.
Defective magnets	Replace the magnets.
Selective resistor is set incorrectly	Check for correct resistance setting to avoid too much resistance.
Grease or brake fluid on the brake lining	Replace the seals or dust caps and the brake lining. Check for leaking wheel cylinder.
Misaligned or bent backing plate	Straighten or replace the backing plate.
Unlike voltage systems	If the tow vehicle has a 6 volt electrical system then use 6 volt magnets.
Short circuit in the electrical system	Check the electrical system with an ammeter.
Poor ground	Check for correct grounding in the tow vehicle, trailer and the connector. Install a ground wire between the tow vehicle and the trailer.
Use of the trailer brakes only	Use of the trailer brakes only, can cause early fade which is loss of friction due to excessive heat. Synchronize the braking through the resistor or controller adjustments and settings.

Brake Troubleshooting Chart (cont.)

Problem: Weak Brakes

Probable Cause	Solution
Wrong wire	Install heavier gauge wire.
Extreme trailer loading	Lighten load, or add a 4 brake system to tandem axle trailers.

Problem: No Brakes

Probable Cause	Solution
Bad magnets	Check with a test light. Replace if necessary
Defective resistor	Check for loose connections or replace.
Poor brake adjustment	Adjust the brakes.
Open circuit	Check for broken wires, loose connections, improper grounding, and a faulty connector plug between the car and the trailer.
Improperly wired or inoperative controller	Check the controller operation with a test light.
Short circuit	Check the electrical circuit.
Loss of brake fluid	Check for leaking connections and wheel cylinders. Also look for a possible hole in the brake line.

Problem: Intermittent or Surging of the Brakes

Probable Cause	Solution
Out of round drums	Rebore the drums if they are more than 0.015 in. out of round.
Loose wheel bearings	Adjust the wheel bearings, replace if they are defective.
Deficient trailer ground	If the ground is through the hitch then install a ground wire.
Broken or loose magnet wires	Check the magnets with a test light and replace if necessary.

Problem: Dragging Brakes

Probable Cause	Solution
Brakes are adjusted incorrectly	Check the brake adjustment.
Electrical defect in the controller	Not enough gap between the controller contactor strip and the coil may cause the brakes to be on continuously.

Brake Troubleshooting Chart (cont.)

Problem: Dragging Brakes

Probable Cause	Solution
Hydraulic defect in the controller or the master cylinder of the tow vehicle or the trailer (surge brakes)	Too much residual pressure in the tow vehicle hydraulic system or a gummed-up controller cylinder may cause the controller to be held "on" slightly. Also a gummed-up master cylinder on the tongue of a trailer equipped with surge brakes would have the same effects as mentioned above.
Corroded brake unit	Check the operation of all unit parts to be sure that they all move freely. Clean and lubricate brake assemblies.
Broken or weak shoe return springs	Check and replace if necessary.
Bent backing plate	Straighten or replace.

Problem: Noisy Brakes

Probable Cause	Solution
Loose parts	Check springs, rivets, bolts etc.
Improper bearing adjustment	Check for damaged or worn bearings. Replace if necessary. Adjust the bearings.
Grease, oil, or brake fluid on the brake linings	Replace the lining and clean the drum.
Lining is worn to the rivets	Replace the linings.
Bent backing plate	Straighten or replace.
Brake release, poor adjustment	A certain amount of noise is normal when the brake releases. Proper adjustment will minimize this noise.

7 · Routine Maintenance and Troubleshooting

Maintenance

Use the following list as a chart for periodic maintenance to the trailer.

1. Lubricate the locking mechanism of the hitch coupler. Also use a small amount of grease on the hitch ball to prevent noise during towing.

2. Make certain that the tires are properly inflated to the recommended pressure. This is critical to the stability and the braking ability of the trailer. It also affects the wear of the tires. Since the trailer wheels are of a small diameter, they sometimes turn twice as many revolutions as the tow vehicle's tires. If the tow vehicle is traveling at 60 mph, the trailer wheels are traveling at 120 mph.

3. If the trailer was packed in either wet or damp weather, you should open it and allow it to air out before packing it permanently. Mold will form on damp canvas and cause deterioration of the material.

If spots of mold have formed on the canvas, scrub it with soap and water and allow the surface to be exposed to direct sunlight. Make certain that the surface is thoroughly dry before repacking the canvas.

If the canvas is beginning to absorb water, spray a water-repellent compound onto the leaking area, allow it to dry, and apply it once more. This compound can be purchased from any good trailer supply store.

4. Aluminum zippers should be lubricated with candle wax or special zipper lubricant, because they will annodize—especially near salt water—which will cause rough operation. Never use oil; this will stain the canvas.

5. Check the torque on the wheel lug nuts before any extended trip. These nuts can loosen during high-speed operation, allowing the wheel to come off. Check with your particular manufacturer for the recommended torque on these nuts. Also make frequent checks of the tire wear pattern. (See the tire section under "Tow Vehicles.") This can be the first sign of loosening lug nuts.

The trailer bearings should also be examined at least twice a year and even more frequently if the trailer is used a great deal. (See "Chassis Maintenance.") Use good bearing lubricant when packing the bearings and also examine the races for wear or scoring and the roller of the bearing for chips.

6. Some trailers have bolts to hold the coupler to the trailer tongue. Check the torque on these bolts to see that they are

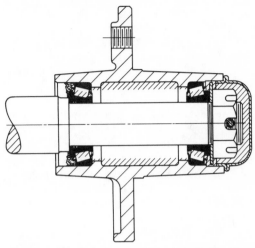

Cross section of the inner and outer trailer bearings

tight and that the assembly is one secure unit.

7. Examine the path of the wiring under and through the trailer to guard against short circuits. Check the wire insulation and the condition of the rubber grommets which separate the wire from metal surfaces.

8. Examine the condition of the gas line (if so equipped) and the security of the connections.

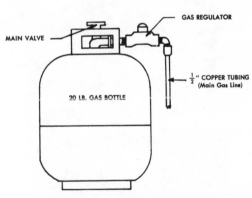

Tubing connections on the gas bottle

9. Lubricate the sliding bed tracks. This will ease movement when the assemblies are folded out. Do not overlubricate, however; only a small amount is necessary.

10. The lifting mechanisms of folding campers should receive some attention. Either check with your dealer or just plain get yourself dirty, but find out exactly how the thing works. Once this is done, you will have located the places where metal

Opening the trailer for airing

contacts metal or other points of wear which may need lubrication.

There are different types of lifting mechanisms; one in particular is a cable type, while another is a geared unit. The former should be examined for frayed or broken cables while the latter should be checked for broken teeth or other malfunctions. The primary cause of breakage in these lifting mechanisms is not component failure, but rather "strong arm" tactics on the part of the owner. The cranking mechanism is made to be smooth and effortless. If it becomes hard, do not force it. Something is evidently binding, so find the trouble before proceeding.

11. It is a good idea to know the dimensions of your tow vehicle-trailer unit. Trailer height is not as critical as with travel trailers where low bridges could be hazardous, but length can be critical. The "combination length" of the trailer and tow vehicle is regulated by law in some states. Some campgrounds also have regulations regarding single-vehicle lengths

Tow vehicle-trailer overall length measurement

due to their terrain and campsite limitations. While the application of these laws rarely applies to camper trailers, ignorance is no excuse.

12. If your trailer has brakes, listen for signs of brake failure. Make an immediate inspection if they squeak, grab, or make any other strange noises. Don't let the inspection go thinking that the noise will cure itself; it won't. By catching a malfunction early, you can avoid expensive damage and possible injury.

Frequently adjust the parking brake to make sure it can hold the vehicle if necessary.

13. A trailer should have a good spare. It must be mounted securely to the trailer tongue or some other suitable spot. If the spare is in open view and it is necessary to have it locked to prevent theft, make certain that the key to the lock is carried with the trailer at all times. It is no fun finding a hacksaw to cut the securing chain.

Since spare tires are not used frequently, occasionally check the tire pressure in the spare to make sure it has more air than the one you are replacing.

It is a good idea to make a checklist which can be applied to the trailer before each outing. Sometimes trailer owners forget all maintenance; they just hitch and go. Because of their basic mechanical simplicity, camper trailers require only a limited amount of periodic maintenance, but don't forget it. It is necessary.

INTERIOR MAINTENANCE

Fabric Upholstery: Use a foam cleaner. Soap and water will leave water marks in the fabric.

Carpeting: Most of the newer camper trailers use indoor-outdoor carpeting which only needs a limited amount of care. A small 12 V vacuum cleaner will keep the carpets clean at all times. Use a foam cleaner to remove stains.

Lifting mechanism in action

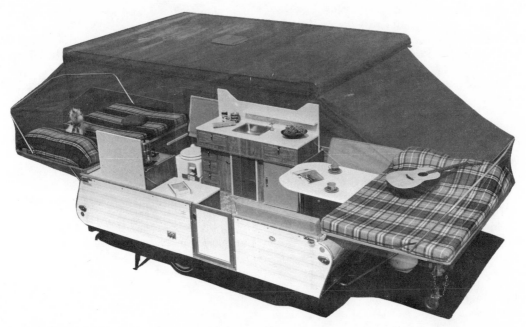

Camper trailer interior

Vinyl Components: Use warm water and soap. Heavy industrial cleaners are not necessary. For routine spills, a damp cloth will work well.

Drapes: Dry cleaning is suggested but consult the fabric manufacturer for their recommendations.

Tables and Counter Tops: Use a mild soap solution. Never use a cleanser as this will dull the finish.

Common-sense maintenance of your camper trailer, in the same manner as for your home and car, will generally give years of trouble-free camping.

CANVAS CARE

Care of the canvas is an important part of the regular maintenance of the trailer. Without maintenance, the canvas may wear out in a relatively short time. If the canvas rips, fix it immediately as it can only grow.

There are two types of patch on the market: the conventional sew-on type, which works best when applied with a heavy-gauge sewing machine; and the new iron-on type, which can be applied in the manner the name indicates. In either case, a coat of spray water repellent should be placed on both the inside and outside of the canvas after patching. In fact, it is a good practice to carry a container of this sealer at all times in the event of leaks.

Canvas Cautions

Be careful not to catch the canvas top between the body and the top. When packing, protect the canvas from any sharp edges where road vibration can cause possible contact and rips.

Keep the canvas top clean. Never store a dirty, damp, or wet top as mildew is a large cause of canvas failure. Wash the canvas with soap and water. Never use any caustic or abrasive substances on the canvas. Make certain that the canvas is completely dry before repacking the camper.

Some camper trailers use tension bars to

Tension bar location

keep the canvas taut. It is not necessary to obtain the tightest adjustment possible as the tighter the canvas surface gets, the harder it is to close the side zippers. It is even possible to break zippers this way.

The units without the vinyl outside covering on the canvas have a tendency to leak when you brush against them. If this happens, use the spray waterproofing on the inside and outside of the canvas.

Avoid parking under low-hanging tree limbs and power tension lines—for obvious reasons.

CARE OF VINYL

Vinyl is possibly the easiest substance to keep clean. Soap and water used frequently will keep the original luster for many years. Cleansers will cause the loss of the shine and some loss of color.

Glue-on repair patches are specially made for vinyl.

ALUMINUM CARE

Preserving the finish of the trailer is just as important as the finish of the tow vehicle. The trailer can be washed in the same fashion as the car. If a scrub brush is used, make sure the trailer surface is wet and the brush is dipped in a soapy solution. No harsh detergent should be used on the trailer as the abrasives contained in it will scratch the finish. Any oil spots can be removed with Naphtha. *Never* use lacquer thinner on any painted surfaces, however.

Any good automotive wax will preserve the finish.

Aluminum Maintenance

Many newer trailers use aluminum for their exteriors. Several manufacturers use bare aluminum, after the fashion of Airstream, without even painting it. This bright surface keeps the interior of the trailer cooler since it reflects heat and the added weight of paint is saved too. Furthermore, aluminum won't rust and it is light and reasonably strong.

Cracks may appear in a trailer's aluminum skin due to road vibration and trailer stress. If the crack is small, it can be stopped by "stop drilling." This is done by finding the very end of the crack and drilling one hole at each end with a $3/32$ in. twist drill. If the crack is large, the same procedure is used except that the larger crack should be caulked liberally. A dou-

bler plate can be applied over the crack and pop-riveted to the skin. The edges of this plate should be caulked as well.

If the trailer is painted, and defects show up in the aluminum, sand the spot until it is smooth and remove all foreign material. Only paint which is made for use on aluminum should be used; other paints will not bind to an aluminum surface.

POP RIVETS

Pop rivets are used on most current aluminum repairs and they are far easier to install than the conventional rivets which have to be bucked. The pop rivet gun listed is the ordinary type which can be purchased at a good hardware store. The rivets are available in various sizes.

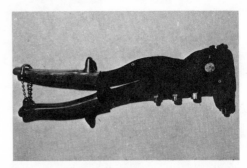

Pop-rivet gun

To use a pop rivet gun, first drill a hole (of the same diameter as the rivet) where the rivet is to fasten. Insert the rivet into the gun with the spiked end entering the gun first. (It is sometimes necessary to lift the handle of the gun when inserting the rivet in order to allow the rivet to catch.) Once the rivet is in the gun, it should stay by itself and the gun handle should be in the cocked position.

Drilling out pop rivets

Place the rivet into the hole where it is to be inserted. Press down on the rivet gun and, at the same time, press down on the gun lever. This will compress the rivet and break off its end so it is flush with its head. If the end does not break off, open the handle of the rivet gun and take another "bite" of the rivet shaft. Push down on the handle until the end of the shaft breaks. Make certain that the rivet is secure because it must be drilled out and another must be inserted if it isn't tight.

DRILLING SOLID RIVETS

Solid rivets, which are used to hold aluminum panels together, are standard equipment on most trailers. If it becomes necessary to remove the panels to gain access to an inner part of the trailer, these rivets must be removed. This procedure is not as simple as it might seem.

First of all, take your time, and if at all possible, use a variable-speed 1/4 in. drill.

Insert a twist drill, of the same diameter as the rivet, into the drill and carefully tap a centering mark in the middle of the rivet's head with a center punch and hammer. Place the tip of the drill into this punch mark and start the drill on a very slow speed, applying a reasonable amount of pressure. Be careful that the drill does not slip from the head and mark the alu-

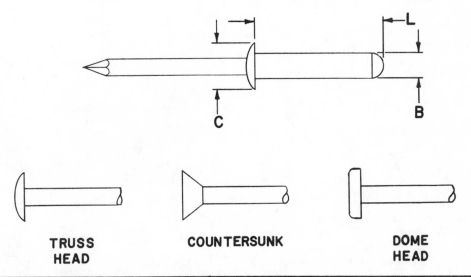

BODY DIA. "B"	HEAD DIA. "C"	HEAD TYPE	LENGTH "L"	GRIP RANGE	HOLE REQ'D.	TYPE
3/16	.342	DOME	.720	.187 — .437	.199	ALUM.
3/16	.336	DOME	.530	.062 — .250	.199	ALUM.
5/32	.255	DOME	.470	.046 — .250	.166	ALUM.
3/16	.625	TRUSS	.656	.250 — .500	.199	ALUM.-GOLD
3/16	.625	TRUSS	11/16	.375 — .500	·.199	STL.
						STL. MAN.
1/8	.250	TRUSS	.419	.251 — .312	.129	ALUM.
5/32	.245	CS	.530	UP TO .312	.166	ALUM.
1/8	.205	CS	15/32	.093 — .250	.136	ALUM.
3/16	.375	BUTTON	25/32	1/2 — 5/8	.199	ALUM.
5/32	.255	DOME	.470	.046 — .250	.166	ALUM.-GOLD
1/8	.215	DOME	.400	.031 — .187	.136	ALUM.-GOLD
3/16	.625	TRUSS	.968	.500 — .781	.199	ALUM.
3/16	.625	TRUSS	.968	.500 — .781	.199	ALUM. DARK

Rivet chart

minum skin. *Do not drill all the way through*. Drill only far enough to spin the head off the rivet. If you do drill all the way through, you will enlarge the rivet hole and necessitate the use of an oversize replacement rivet. Once the head is removed, the remainder of the rivet can be removed from the skin by punching it out with a small drift pin.

Solid rivets are usually replaced with pop rivets because they are so easy to install. This procedure is highly recommended. For pop rivet installation procedures, see the preceding section.

FIBERGLASS REPAIRS

Many trailers have various fiberglass components which, under the stress of towing, either crack or break. It is not always necessary to replace the entire section. The following sections give detailed outlines of how to repair both major and minor fiberglass defects.

Fiberglass repair kits with resin, hardener, thixatrope, fiberglass cloth, and other essentials are available from auto shops which specialize in fiberglass car bodies or boating supply outlets which do fiberglass boat repairs.

Loose-strand fiberglass is used in resin preparation. Since both resin and spun fiberglass can be irritating to skin, apply protective cream to your hands and arms when making fiberglass repairs.

If the fiberglass must be sanded after it is applied, work in the open air or see that the sander being used has a vacuum attachment to collect all of the fiberglass dust.

NOTE: *When working with the resin, mix and apply it in a well-ventilated area; the fumes can be toxic.*

For the repair of minor damage, remove all paint and other coating from the damaged area. Follow the directions, mixing only enough fiberglass to be used in a half hour. Apply the resin with a rubber squeegee or a putty knife. Fill the damaged area, smoothing the fiberglass to the contour, and finish by sanding the area smooth and then repainting it.

Completely cracked or broken panels are classified as major repairs. Before mixing the resin, which is done in the same manner as for a minor repair, remove all the paint from the area surrounding the

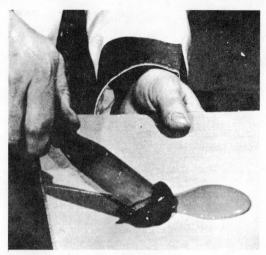

Mixing the resin with the hardener (© Chevrolet Div. G.M. Corp.)

Mixing the finished resin with the fiberglass mat (© Chevrolet Div. G.M. Corp.)

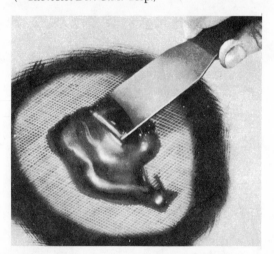

Applying the resin to the damaged area (© Chevrolet Div. G.M. Corp.)

damage. Grind the edges of the damaged area so that they form a wide "V." This will provide a good bonding surface for the resin. For severe damage, coat a layer of sheet fiberglass in the resin and bond the damaged area on both sides.

For scratched panels or spot repairs which have gone through to the fiberglass, it is necessary to remove the paint from the surrounding area. Feather sand the damage with no. 220 or 230 wet sandpaper until it is smooth and level. Do not sand into the fiberglass mesh.

For cracked panels, it is best to work with the temperature of the work area at least 70–75° F. This will ensure sufficient hardening of the resin. To be certain of the conditions recommended, check the resin container for the exact instructions. Use lacquer thinner to remove all paint and

Finish sanding the damaged area

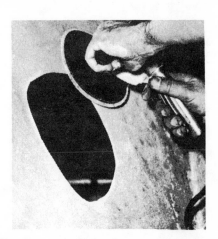

Ruffing the area with a sander

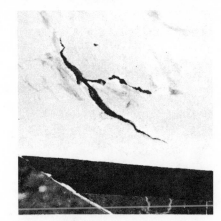

Break in the trailer skin

Reinforcing the damage from the inside of the trailer

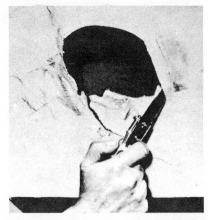

Cutting the loose pieces from the damaged area

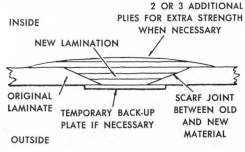

Fiberglass repair construction

foreign material from both the surface and the underside of the fractured section. Rough the surface of the fiberglass to afford a better bonding surface and remove all jagged edges from the fracture, applying a 30° angle to the broken edges. Align the broken panels. This can be done with C-clamps. Follow the outlined procedures under the "Major Repair" paragraph.

Strength of the Repair

If the fiberglass repair is done correctly, the finished product will be as strong, or stronger, than the original surface. Extra strength may be added, as listed in the preceding section, by inserting reinforcing panels constructed of mesh fiberglass that have been dipped in the resin solution and applied to the rear portion of the damage.